Gretchen Grace

TWO WAY STREET

Daylight

Cofounders: Taj Forer and Michael Itkoff
Creative Director: Ursula Damm
Copy Editor: Gabrielle Fastman

ISBN: 978-1-954119-19-2

Printed by Ofset Yapimevi, Turkey

Daylight Books
E-mail: info@daylightbooks.org
Web: www.daylightbooks.org

FOREWORD

For decades, women have been talking about our relative lack of visibility in street photography, and the arts in general. We have always been there, fighting to raise our heads in what has historically been a genre dominated by men, but in recent years, empowered in part by social media, women-only street photography groups and communities have appeared. Women with the drive and determination to support and encourage other women have begun to provide platforms that recognize our talents, instill confidence, increase our visibility as artists, and give room to consider, Is there such a thing as the female gaze? Do women see the street differently? Do we make photos of different things?

In *Two Way Street*, Gretchen Grace offers us two very different visions of her city. Two different ways of seeing and shooting. Two different stories.

One story is familiar. It is constructed from real moments captured of people on the city's streets. We are already familiar with nostalgic black-and-white depictions of New York. Gretchen adds her own happy, joyful, and quirky stories to this visual tradition.

The other story shared in these pages is told in color, through which Gretchen reveals abstract pieces of her city and breaks down its vastness and complexity into compelling vignettes.

Where the two stories and the two sides of the street merge is in the shared vibrancy with which these images collectively convey life in this amazing city.

The early black-and-white work pays homage to the city as it emerged from an era of grime and grit that had (in our imaginations, and in movies, at least) once characterized it. It tells classic stories of life on the streets.

In her abstractions, Gretchen seeks out color, uses the light, and focuses on details that few people would see as they hurry past. But she pauses, and notices the possibilities in a given moment, and extracts a thing of beauty from the apparent simplicity of her scenes.

Her images demonstrate a masterful and intimate knowledge and sensitivity to light and how it works at a particular time on a particular day, at a particular time of the year. And they very much reveal the artist that she is.

As photographers mature, they become either more adaptable or more set in their ways. Adaptability is a gift and Gretchen clearly has it. *Two Way Street* shows us two very different views of New York. Two visions by one artist. Two different stories of a city that we are familiar with, and one that we may not usually see. They are stories of nostalgia, humor, and (de)light. They are vibrant and colorful, simple and complex. They are Gretchen's—of her city and of herself.

—Julia Coddington

TWO WAY STREET
PART I

When you live in the city you walk everywhere, and for me as a visual person, walking means looking. At a certain point I started recording what I saw. Shooting in New York City is like being a kid in a candy store photographically speaking; there is always something to photograph. These photos represent the path of my visual exploration as an artist and the development of my specific language. And in retrospect, my focus has always been the same—finding the iconic moments of the everyday.

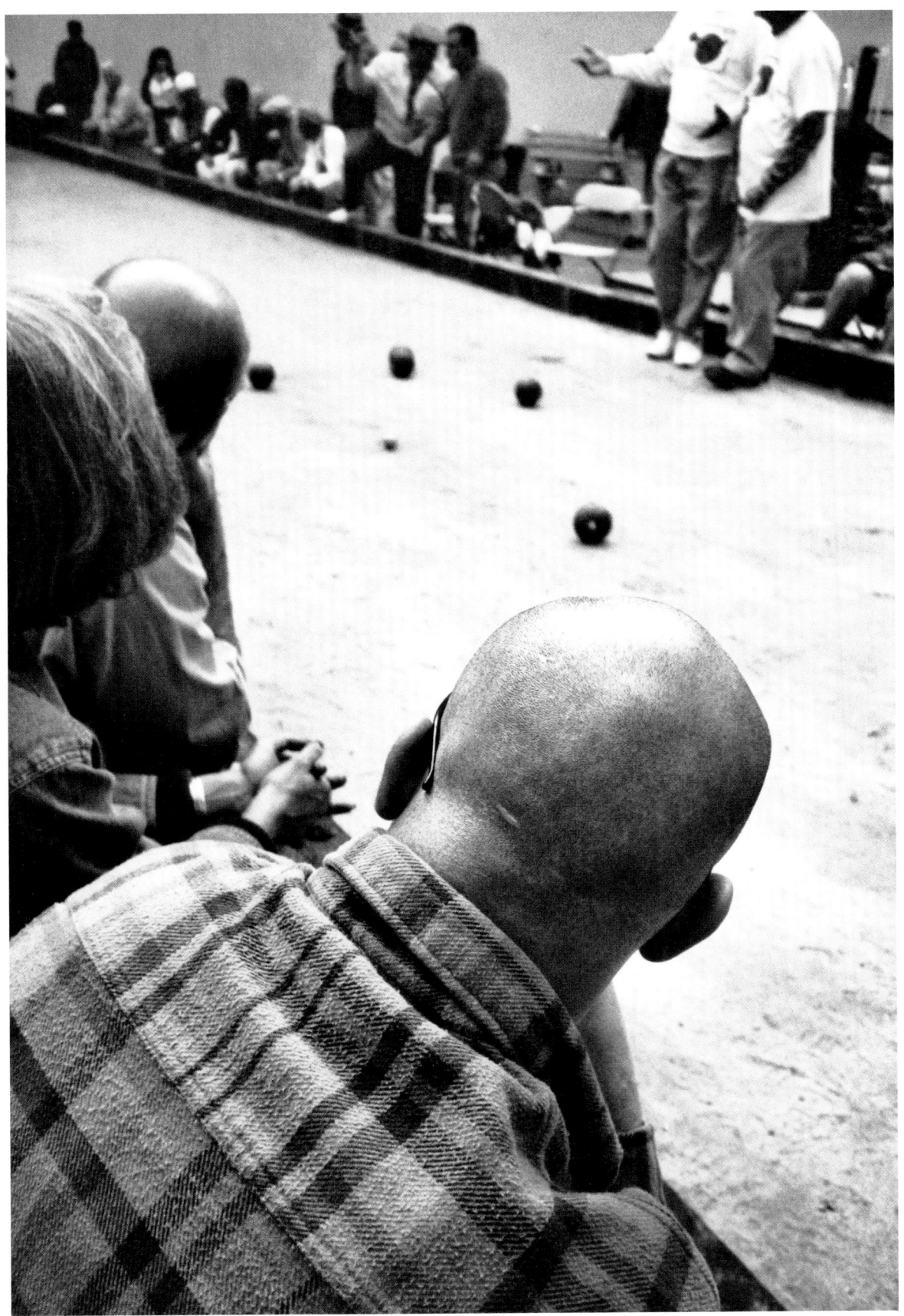

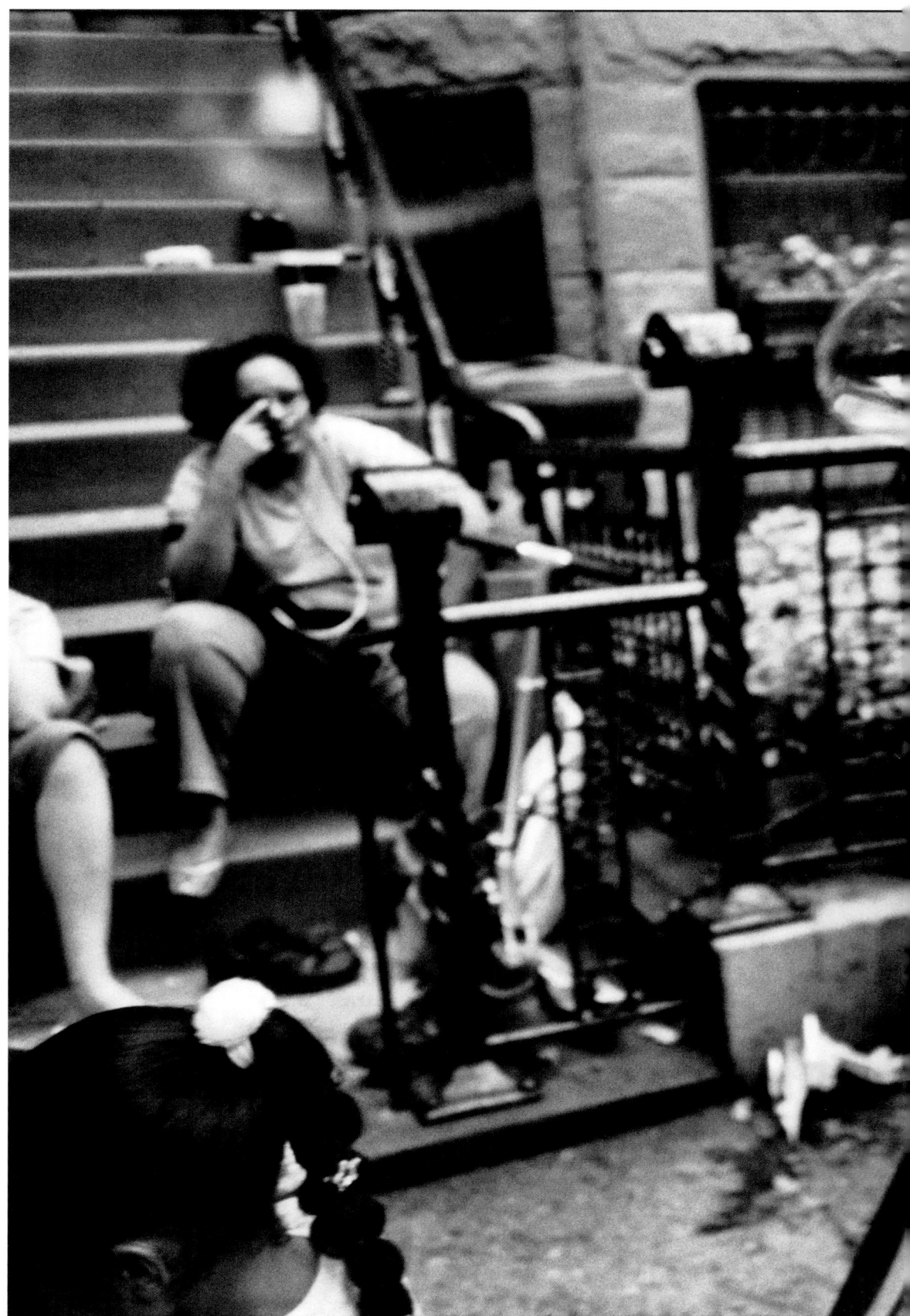

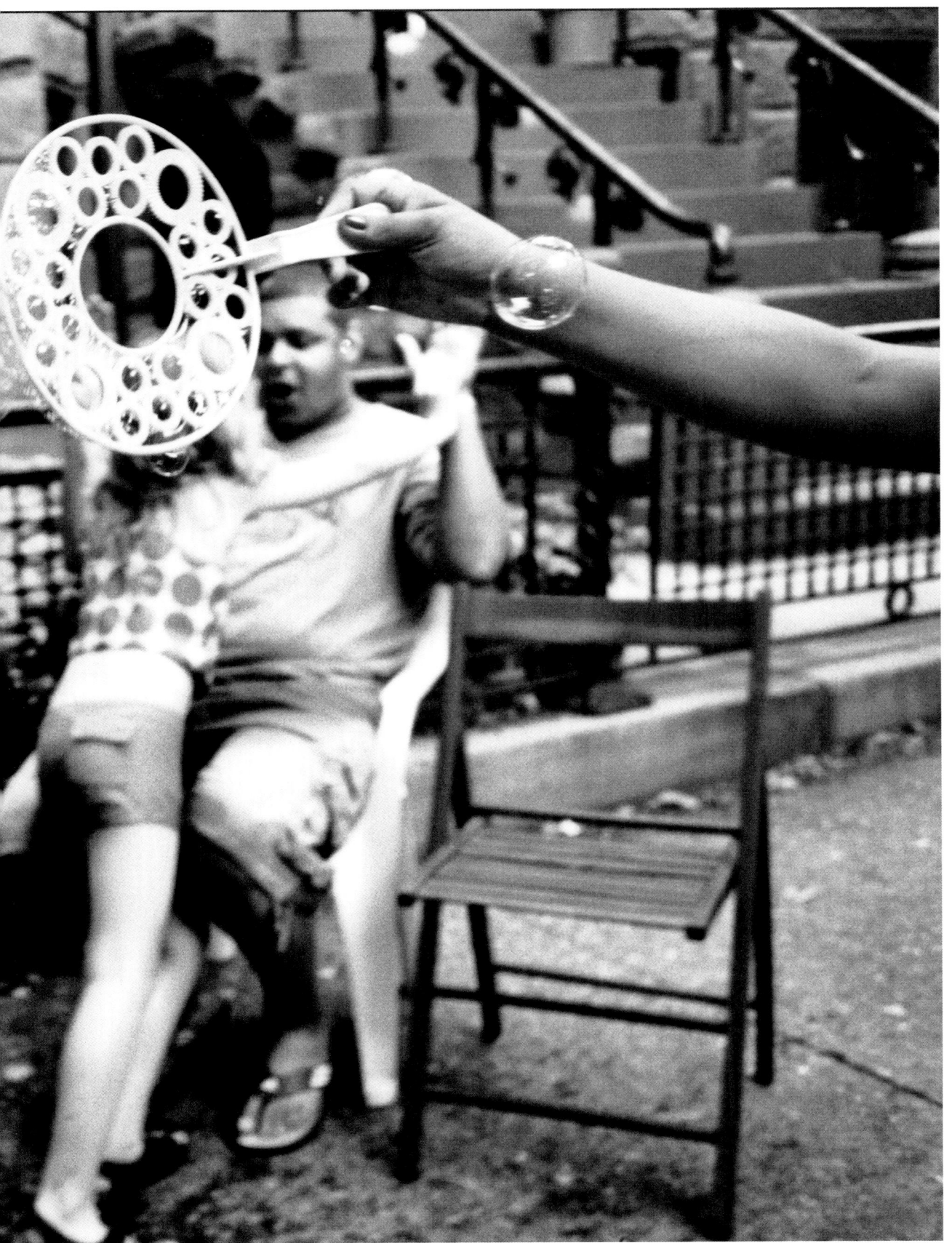

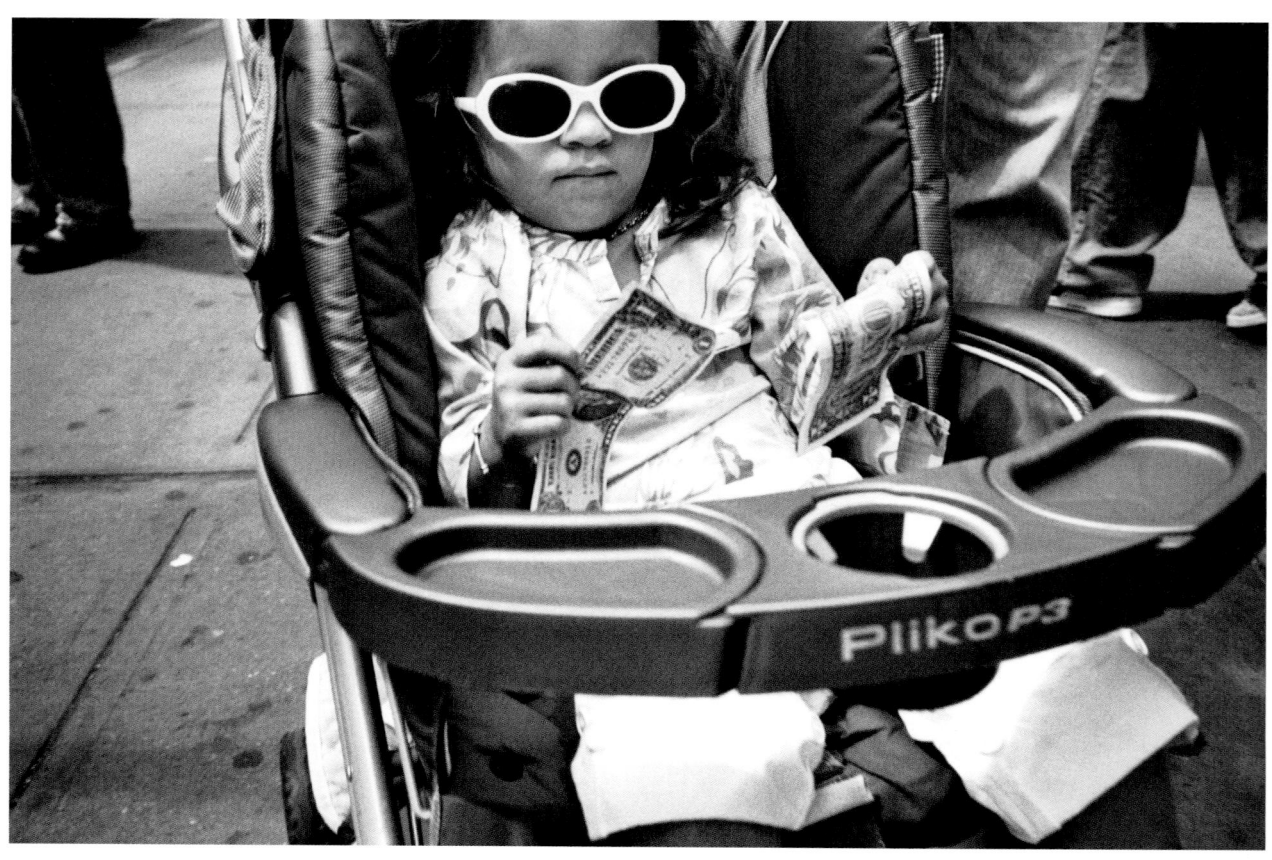

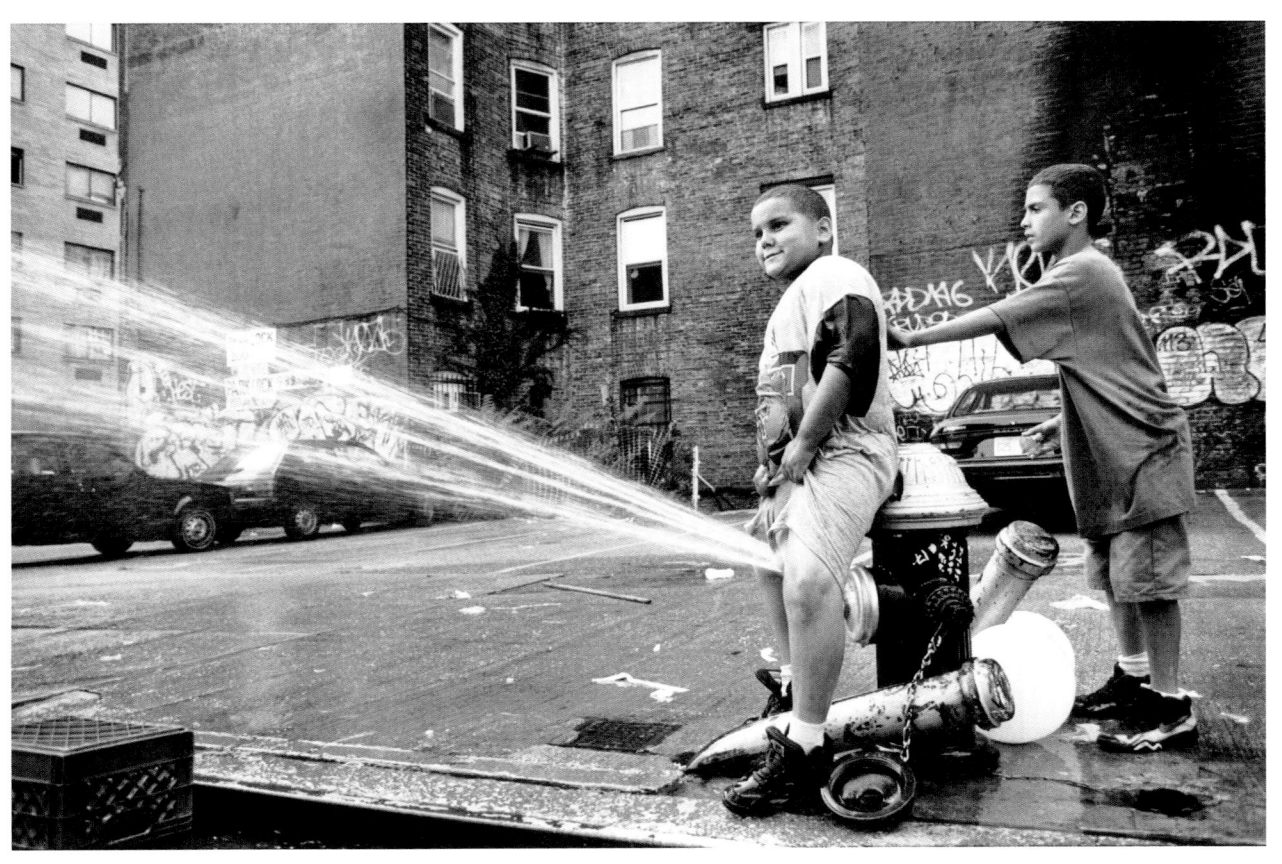

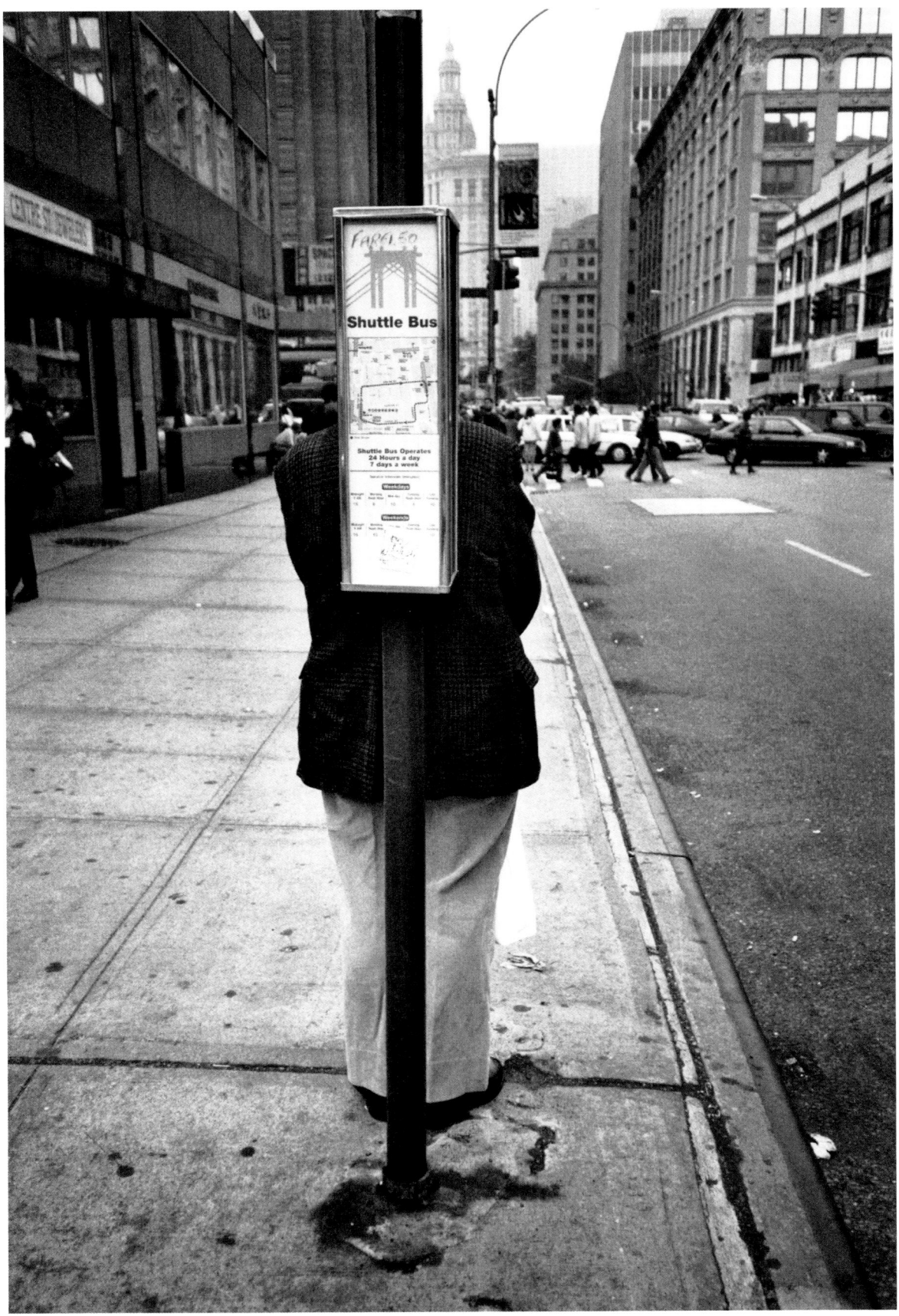

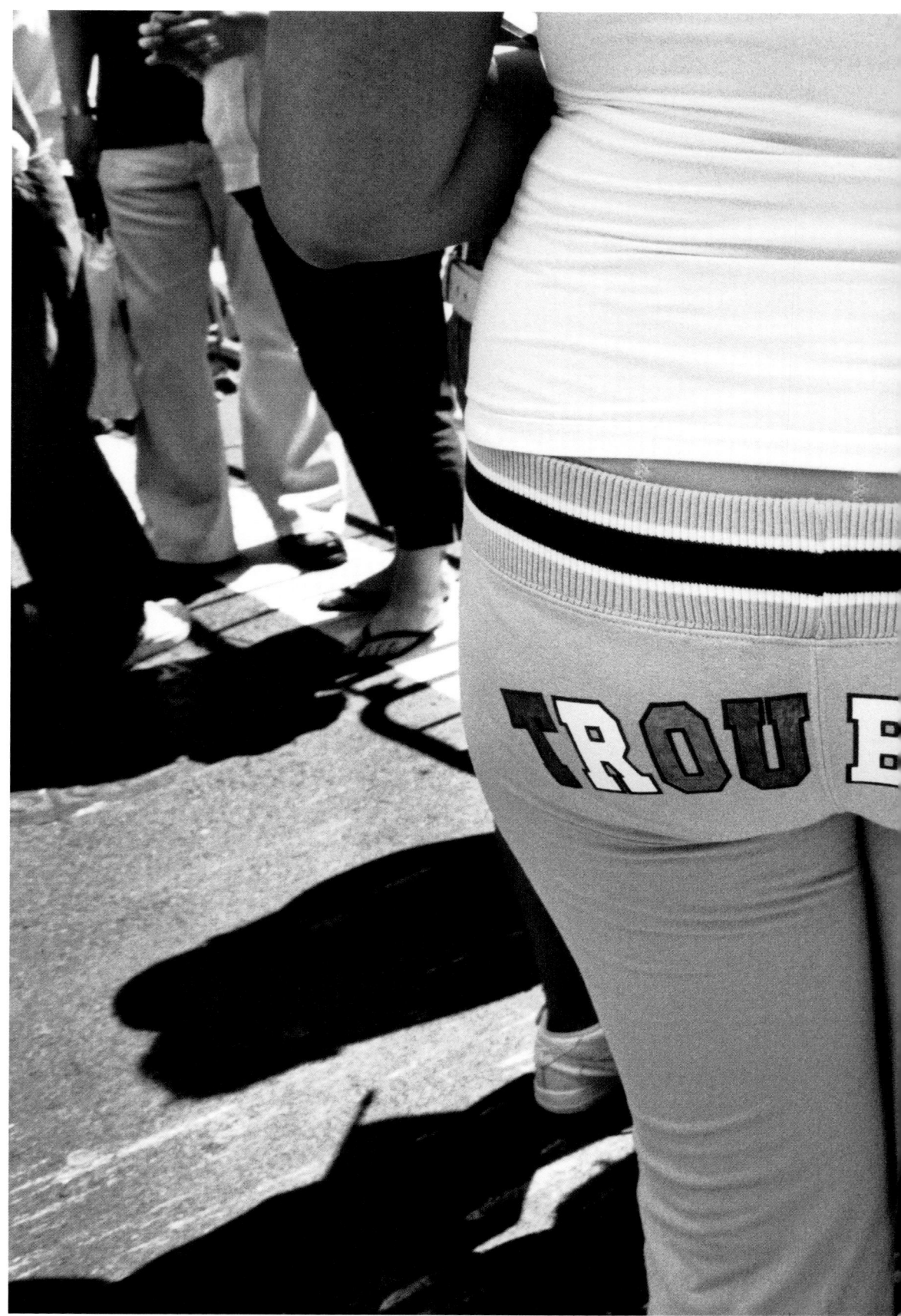

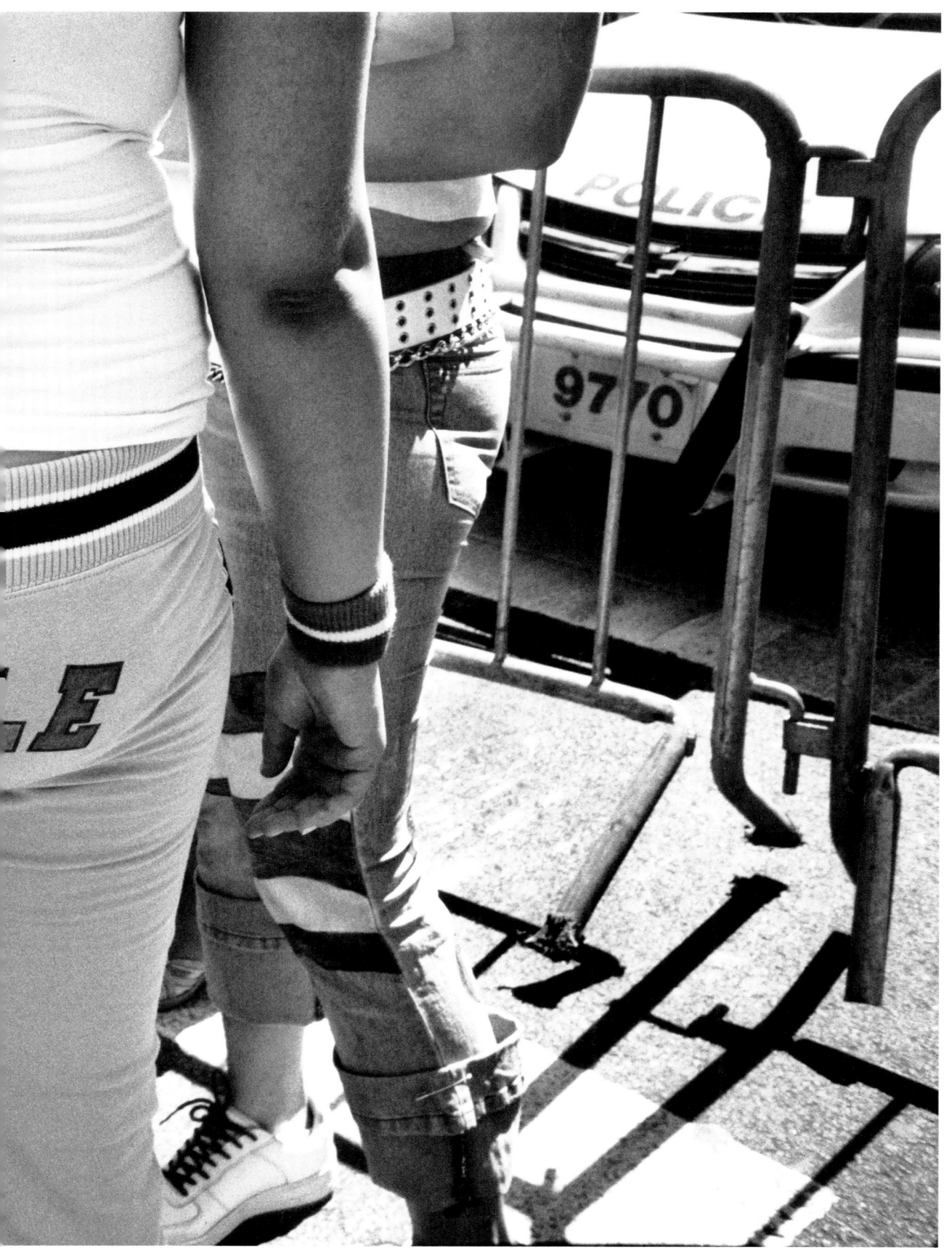

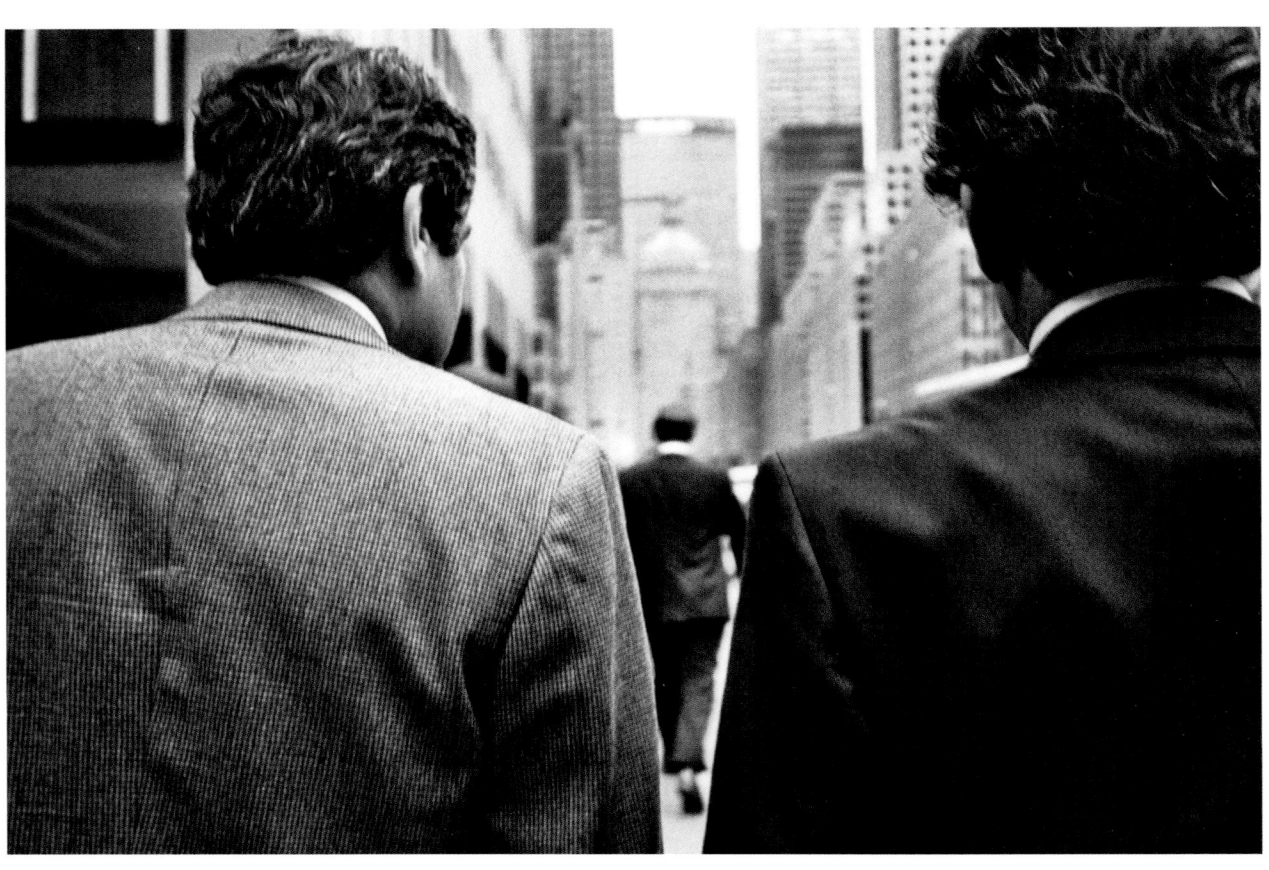

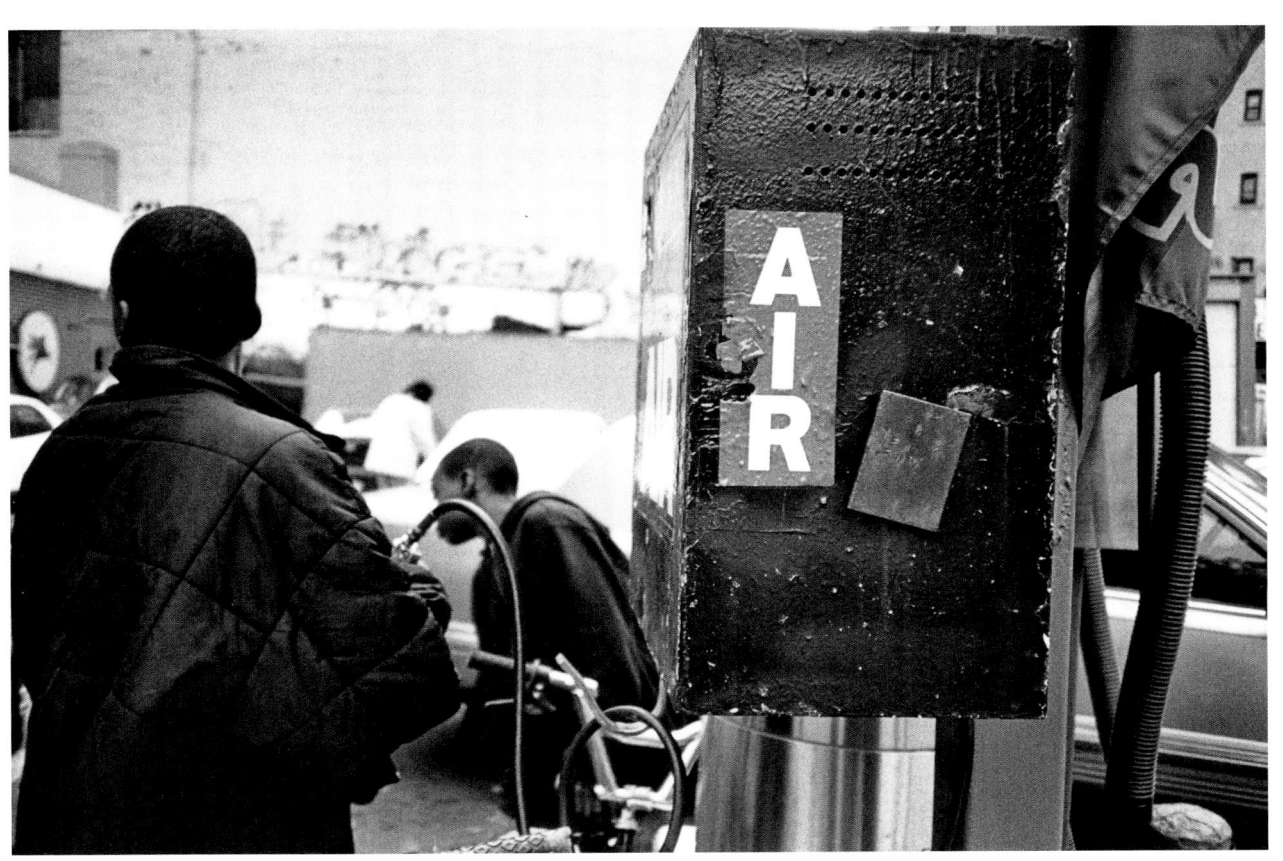

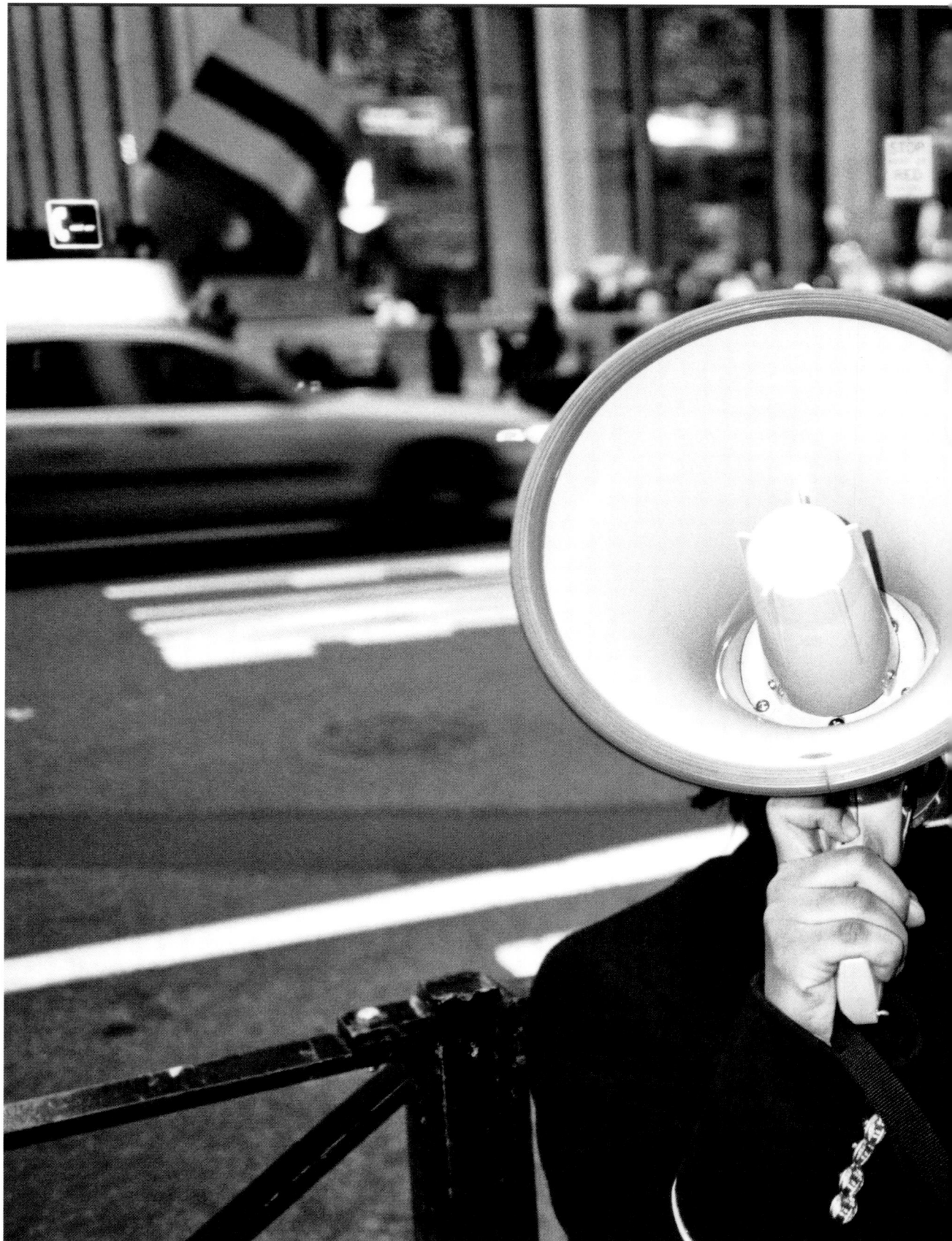

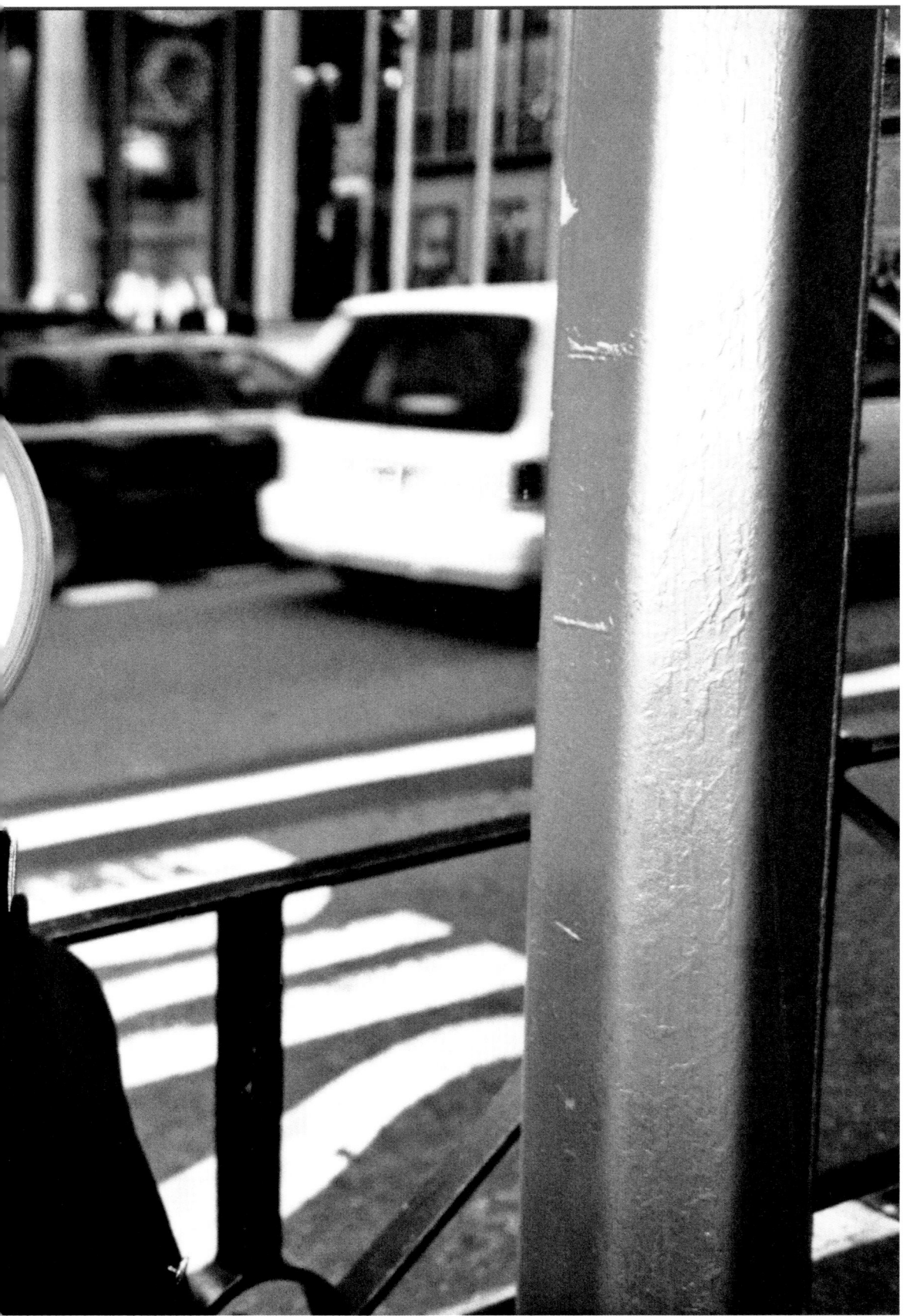

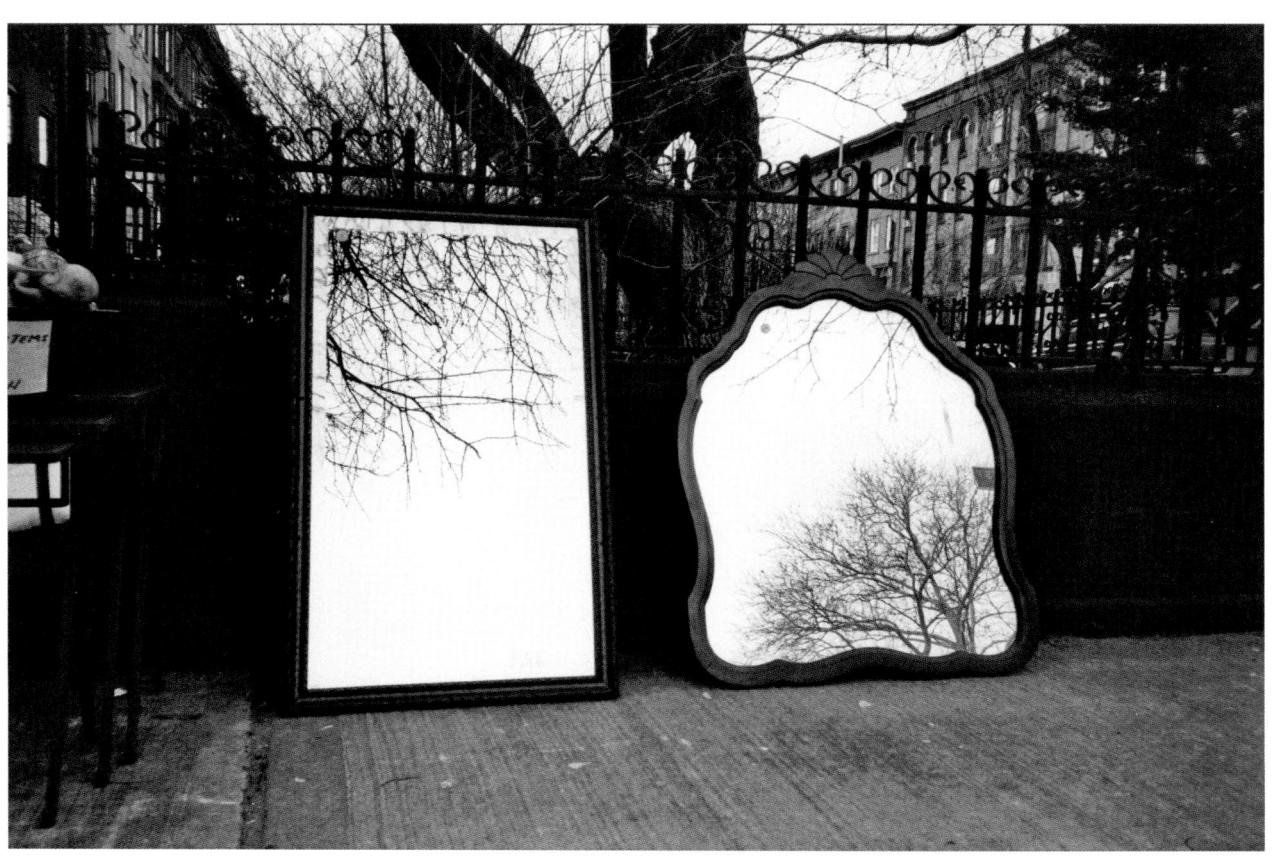

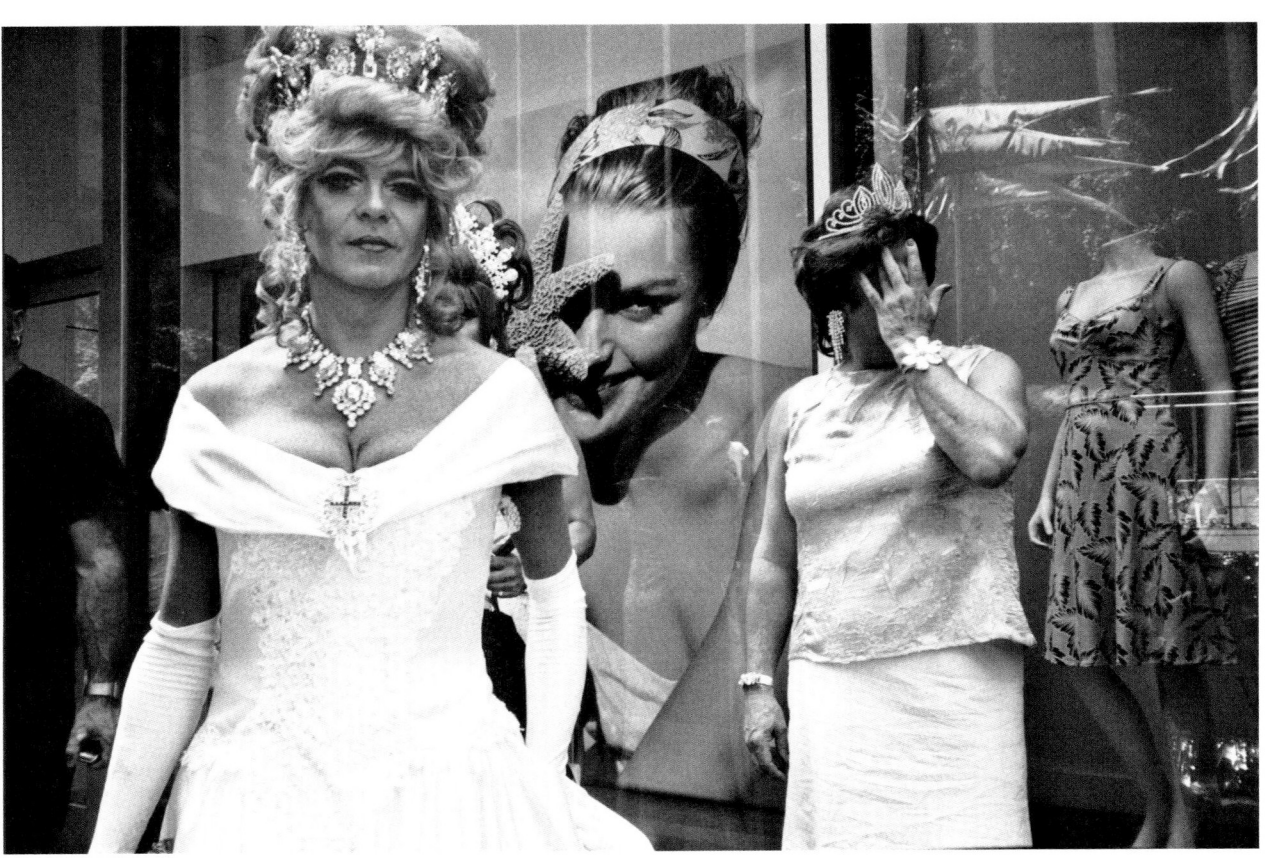

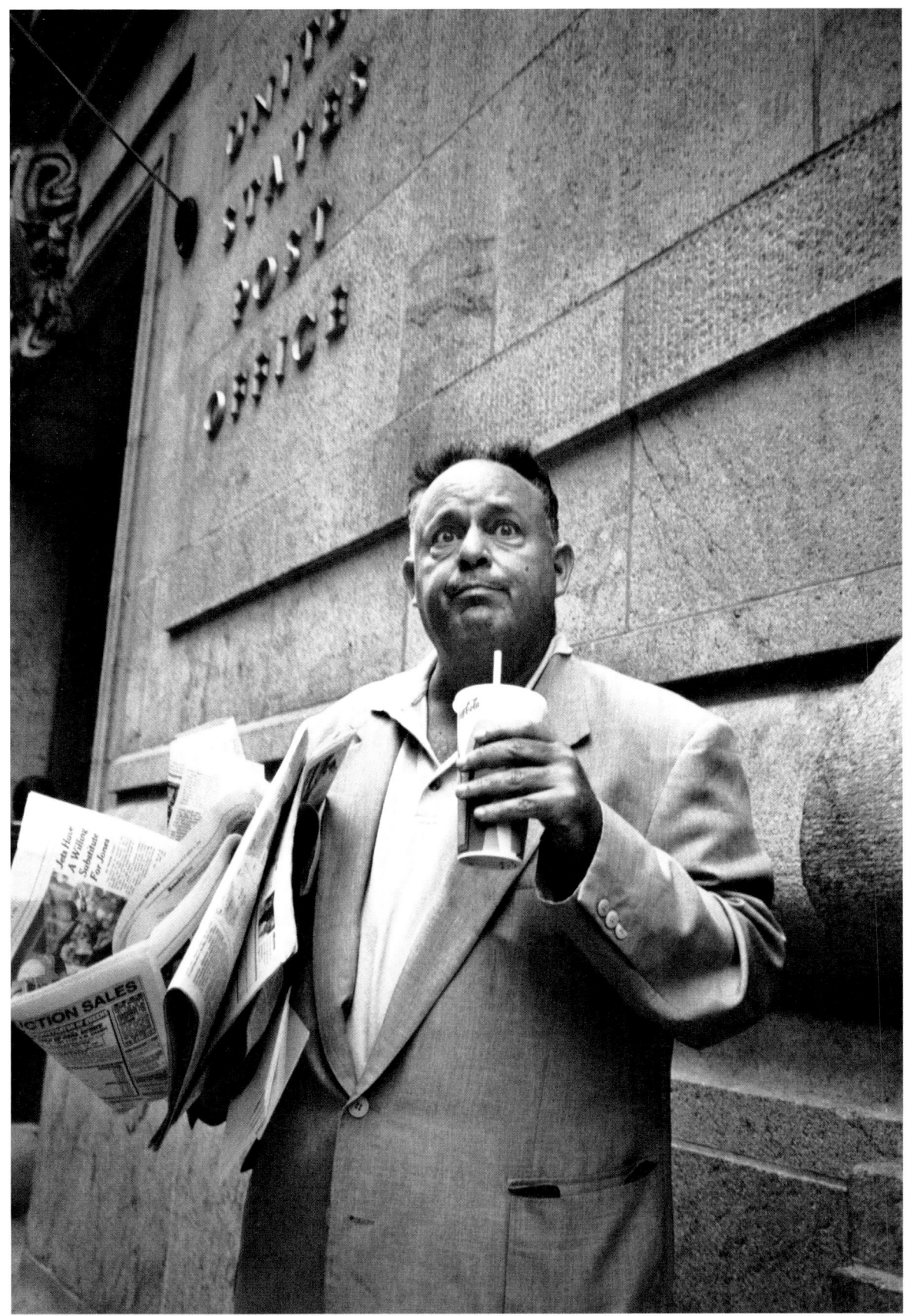

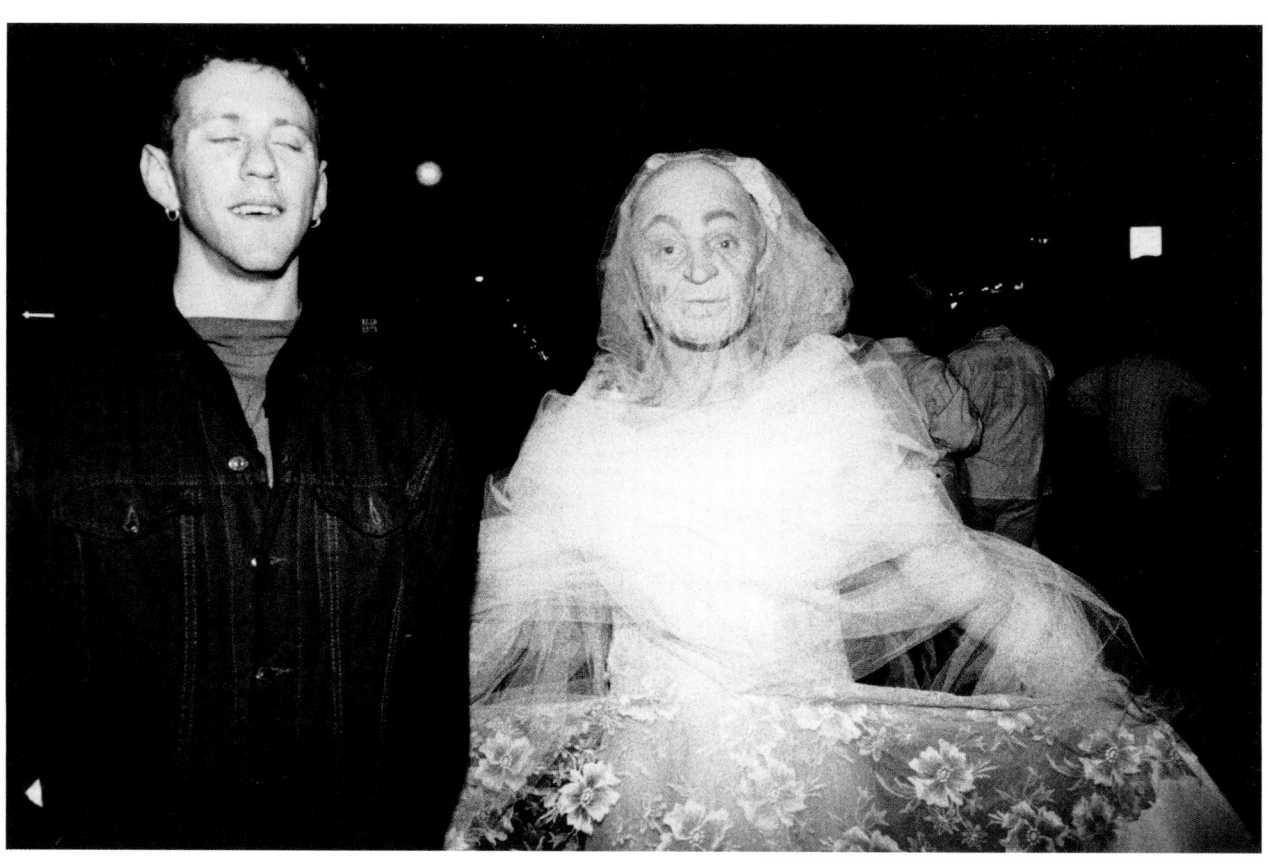

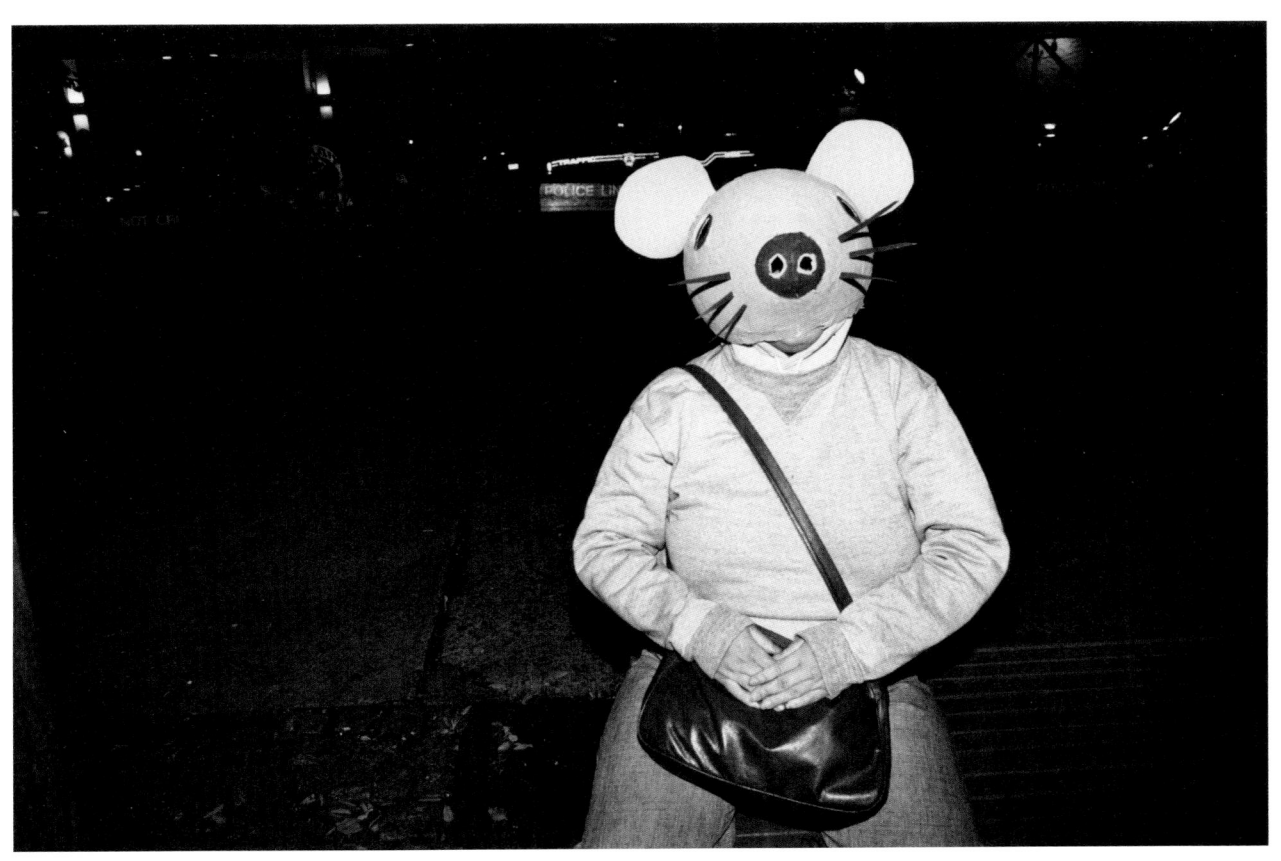

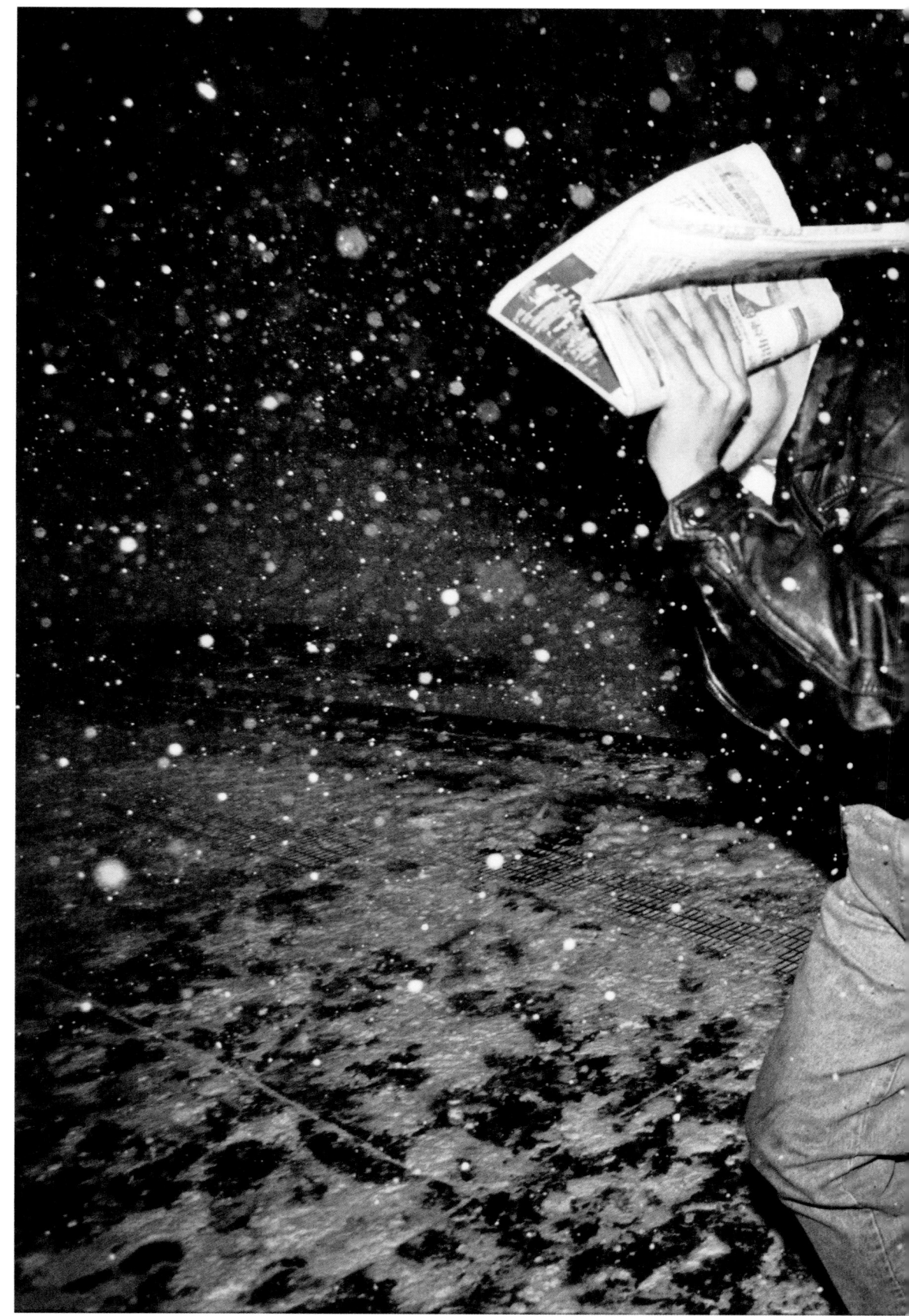

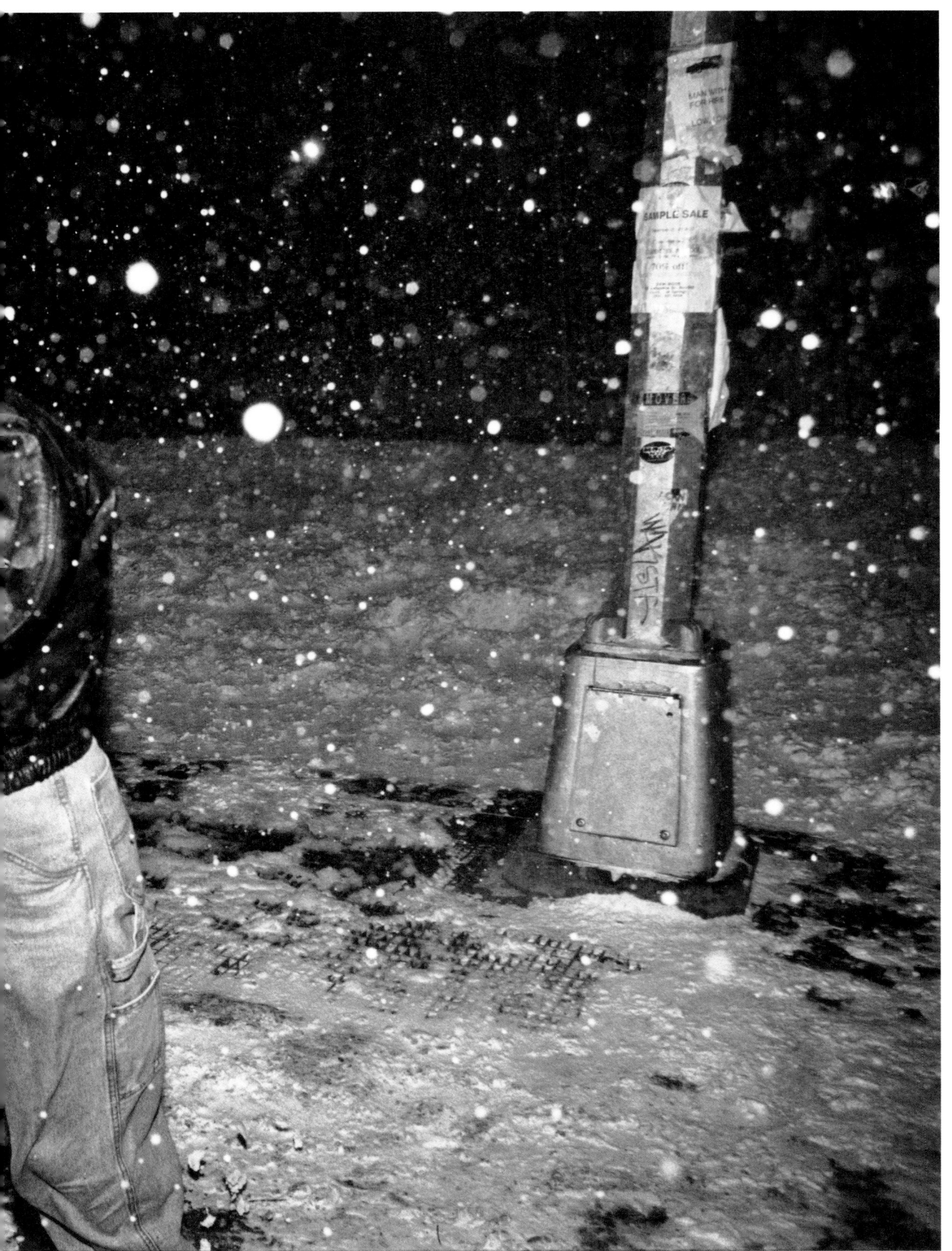

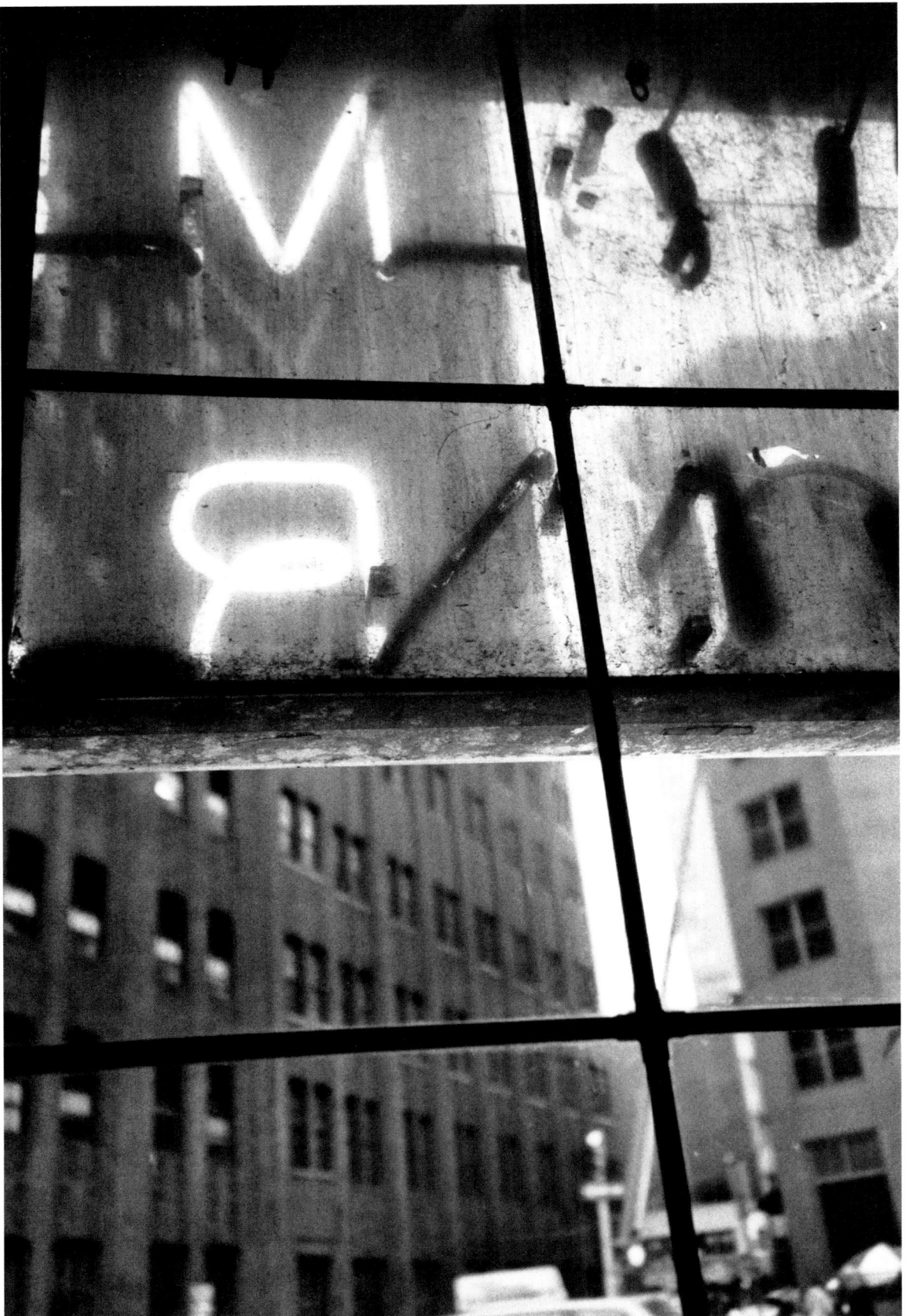

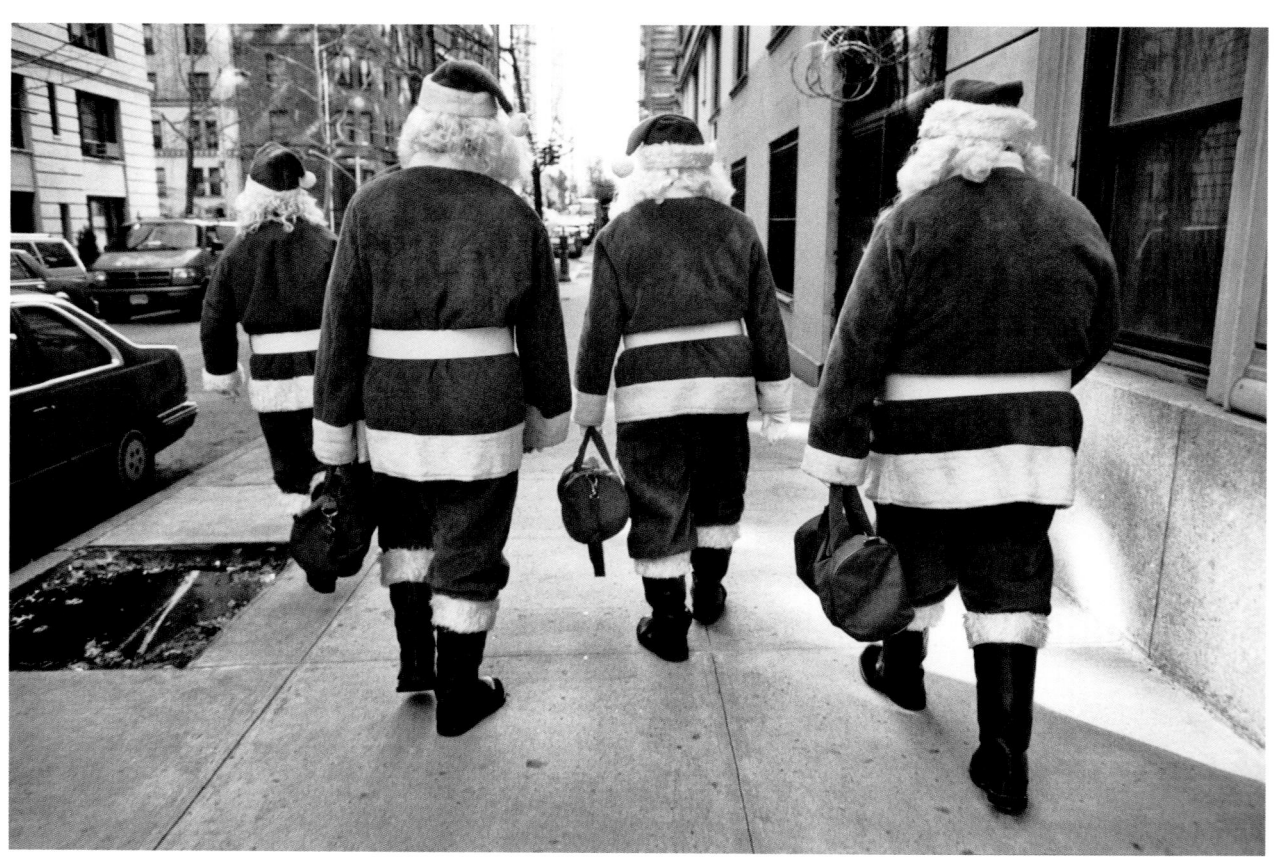

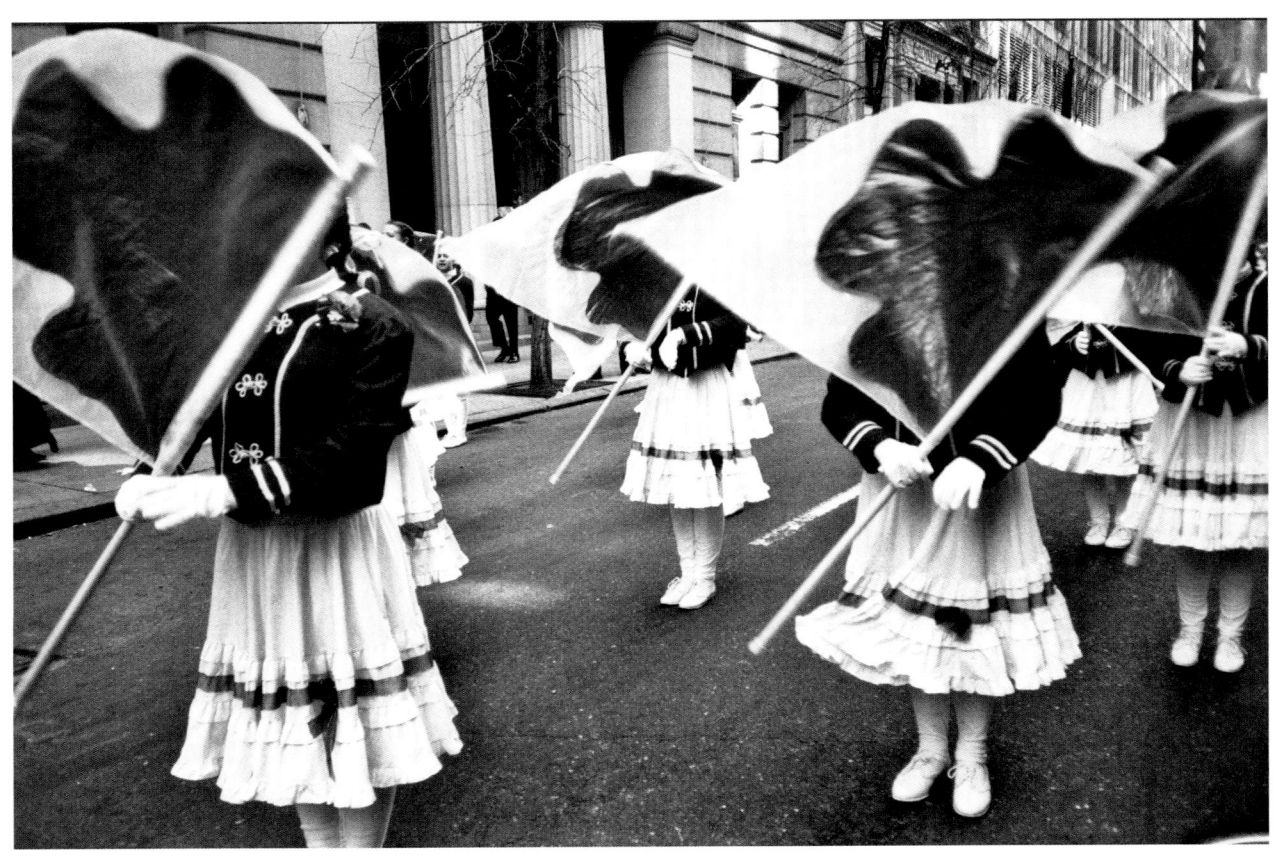

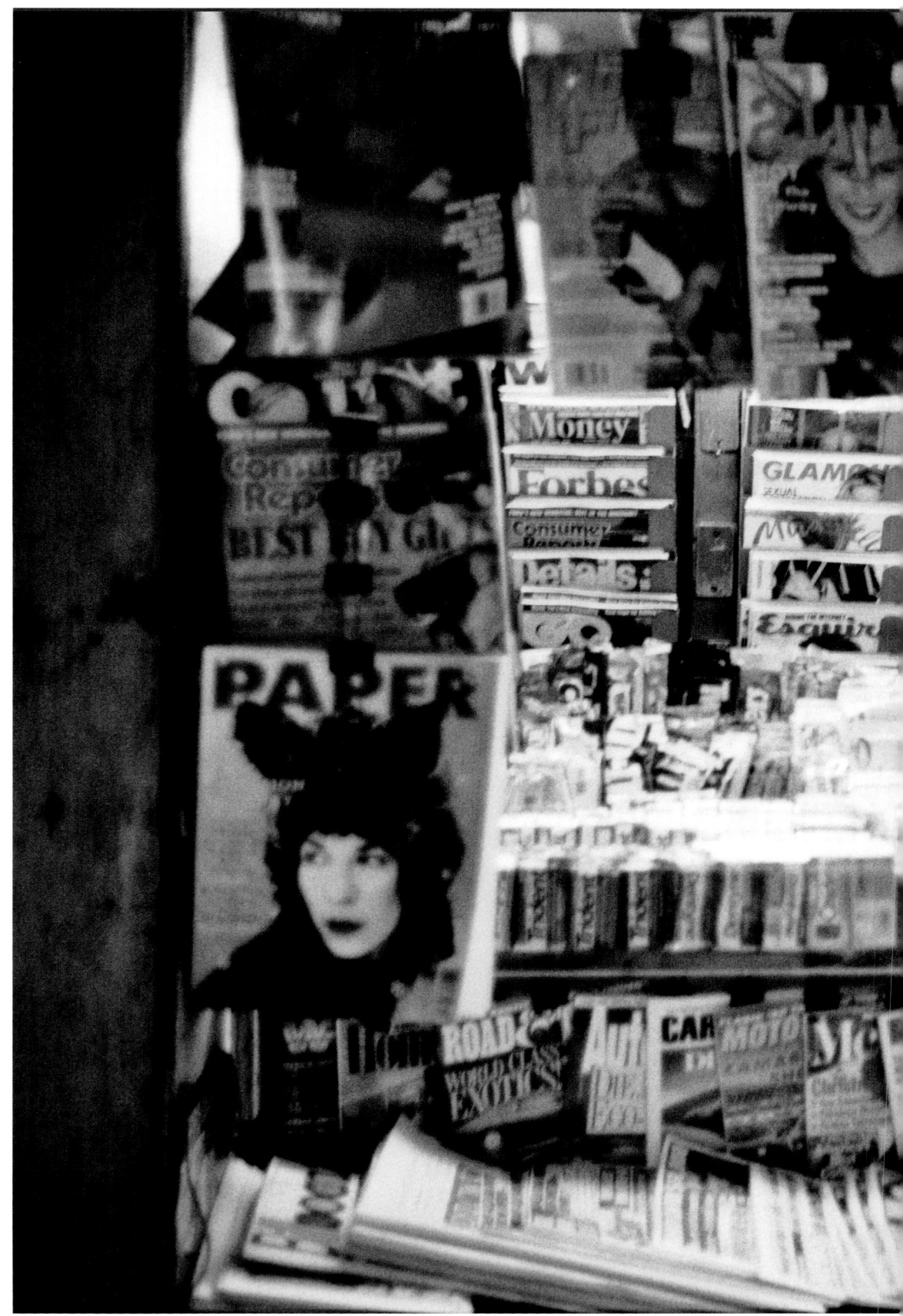

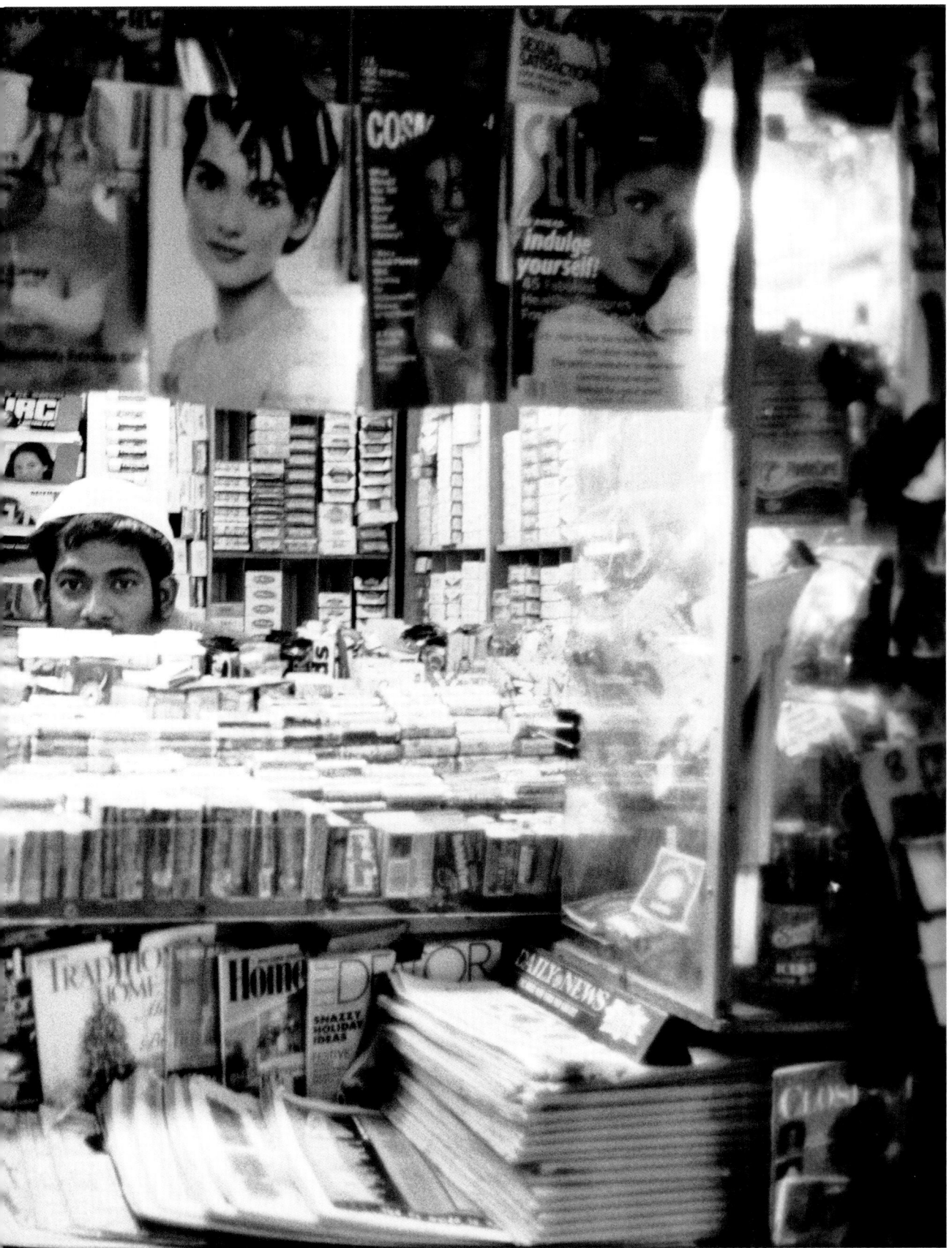

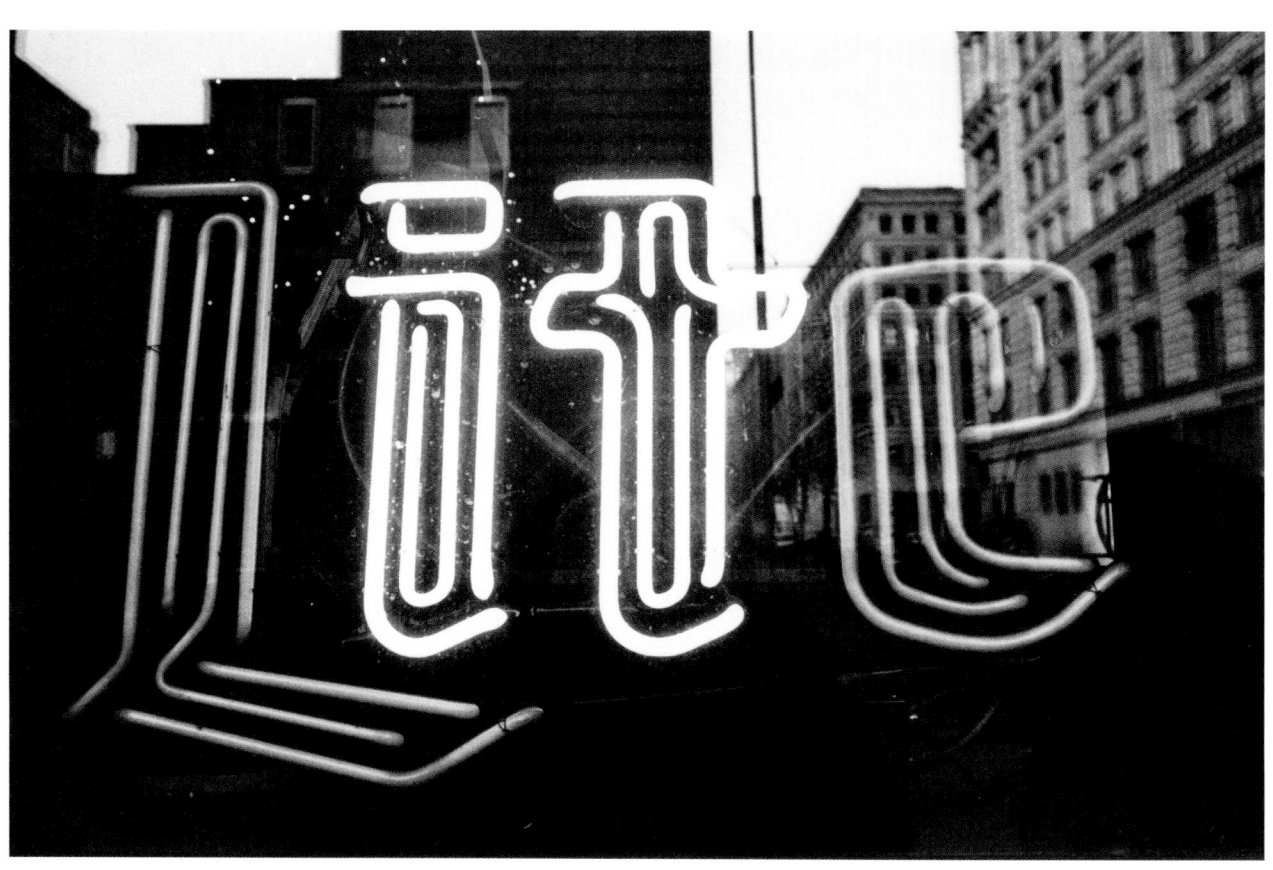

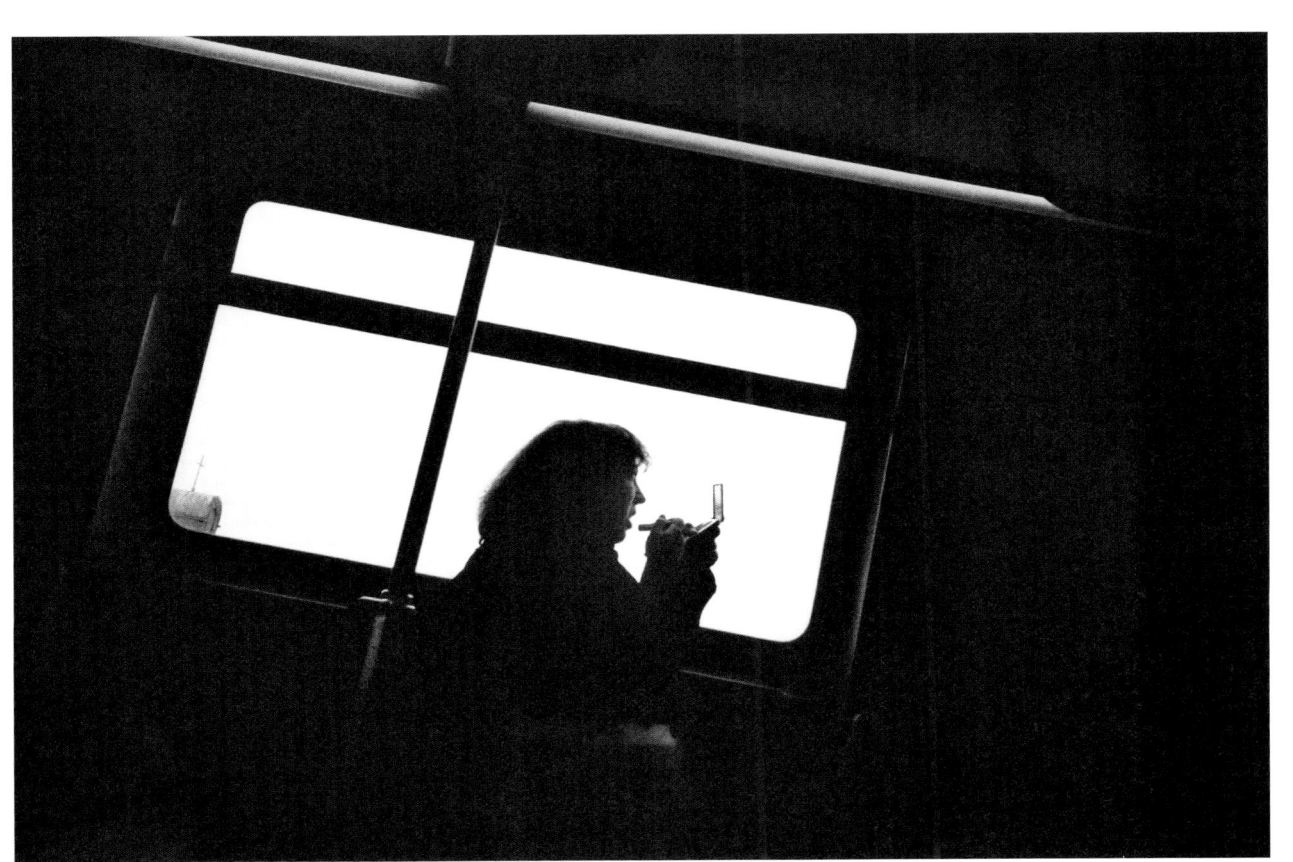

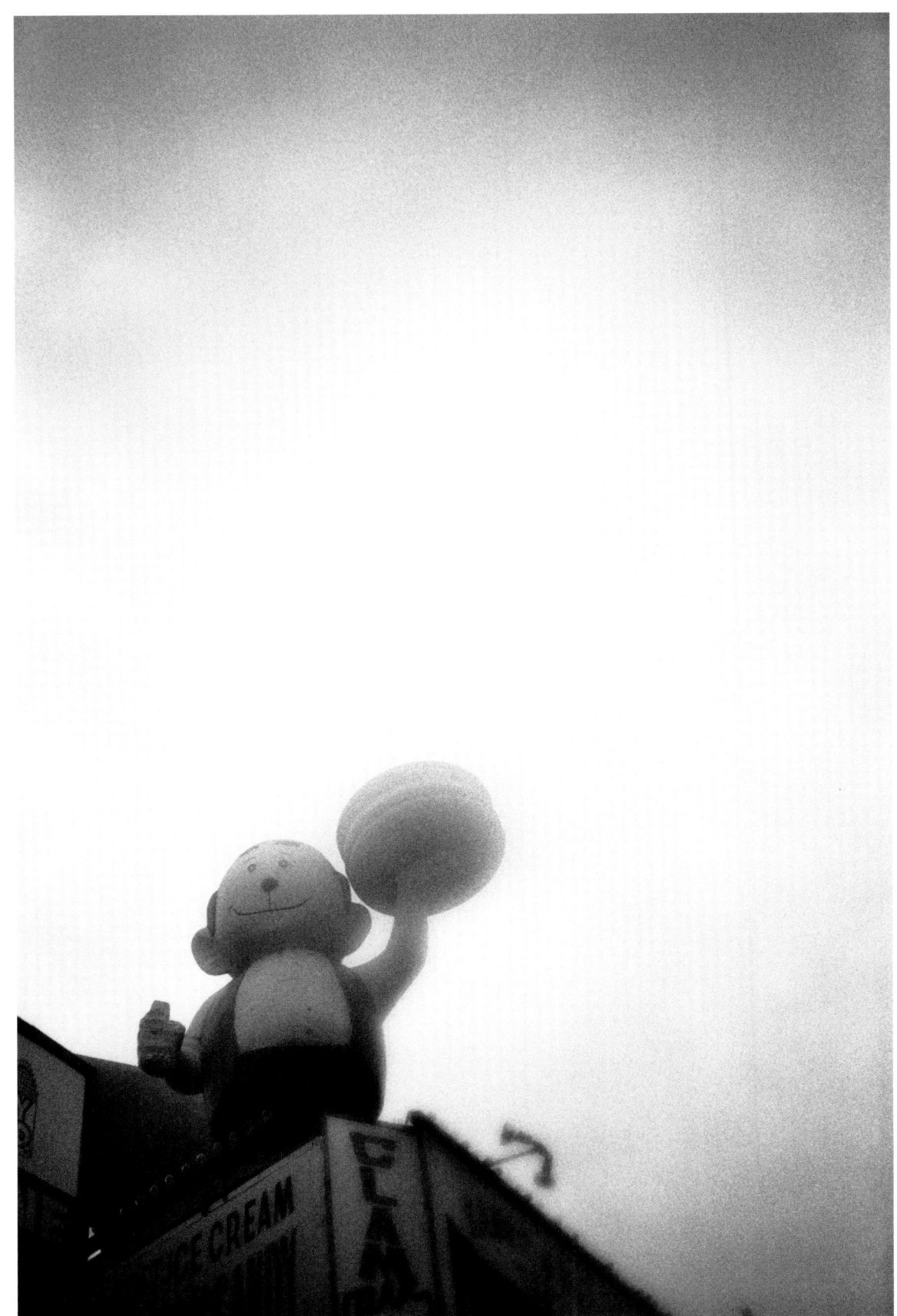

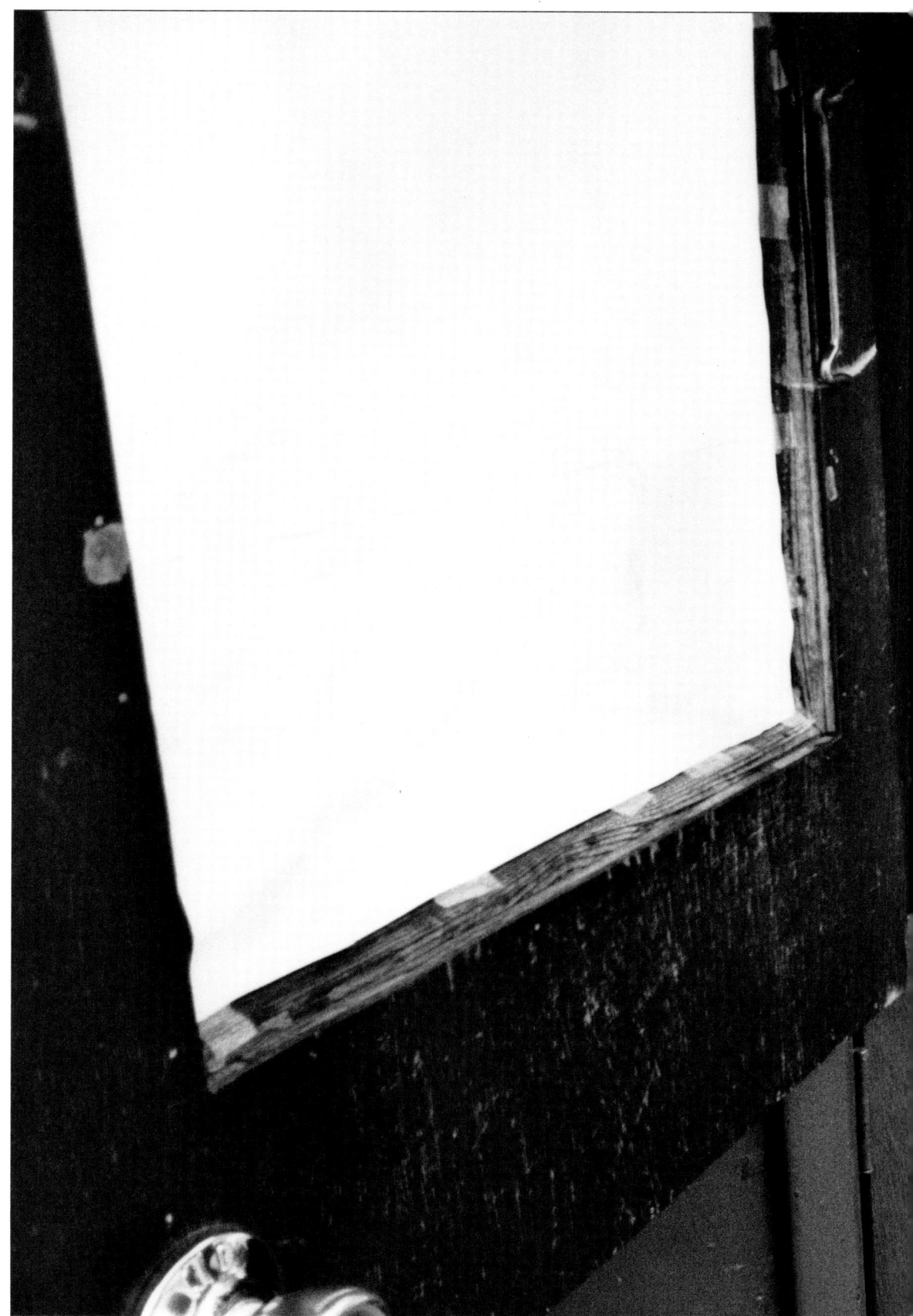

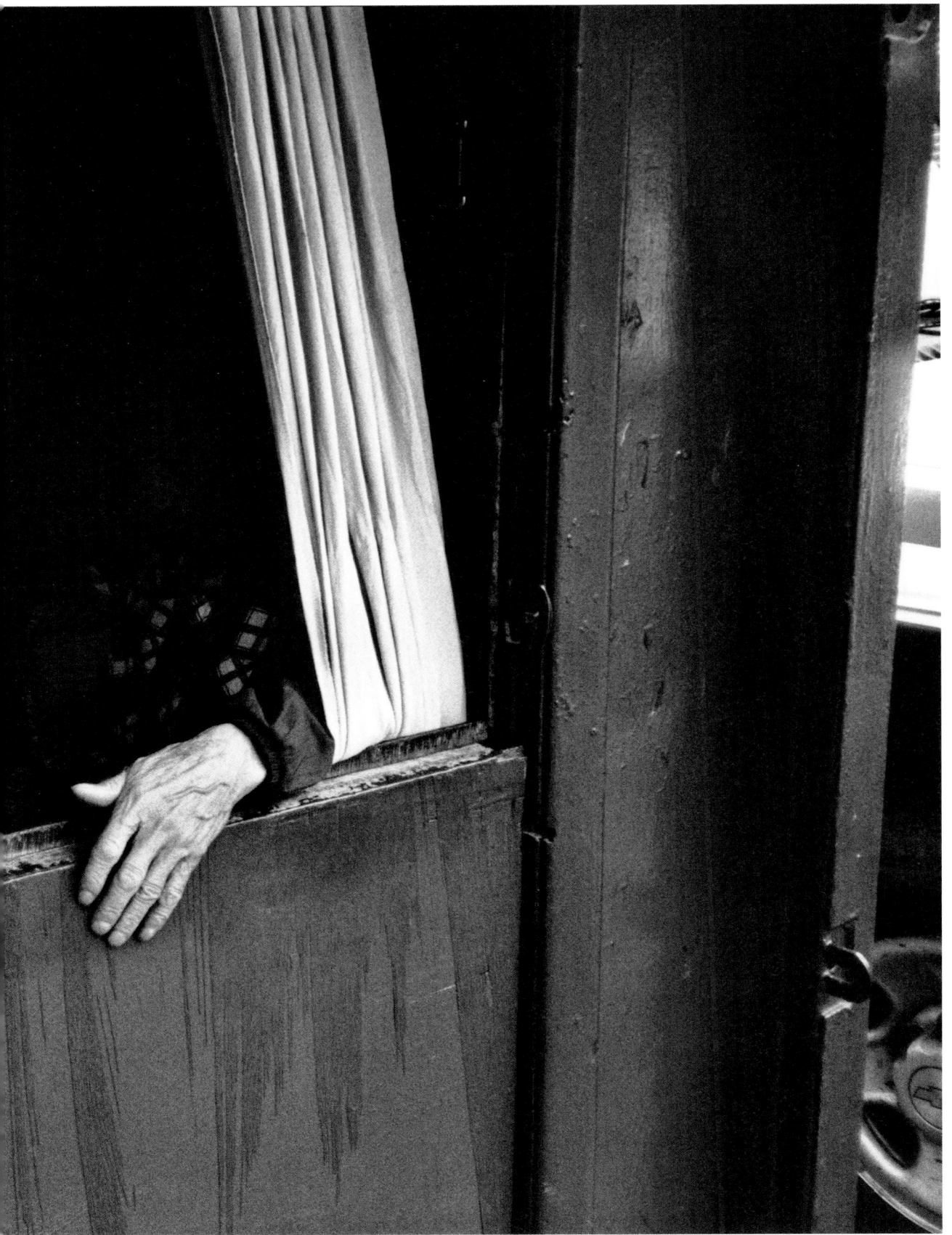

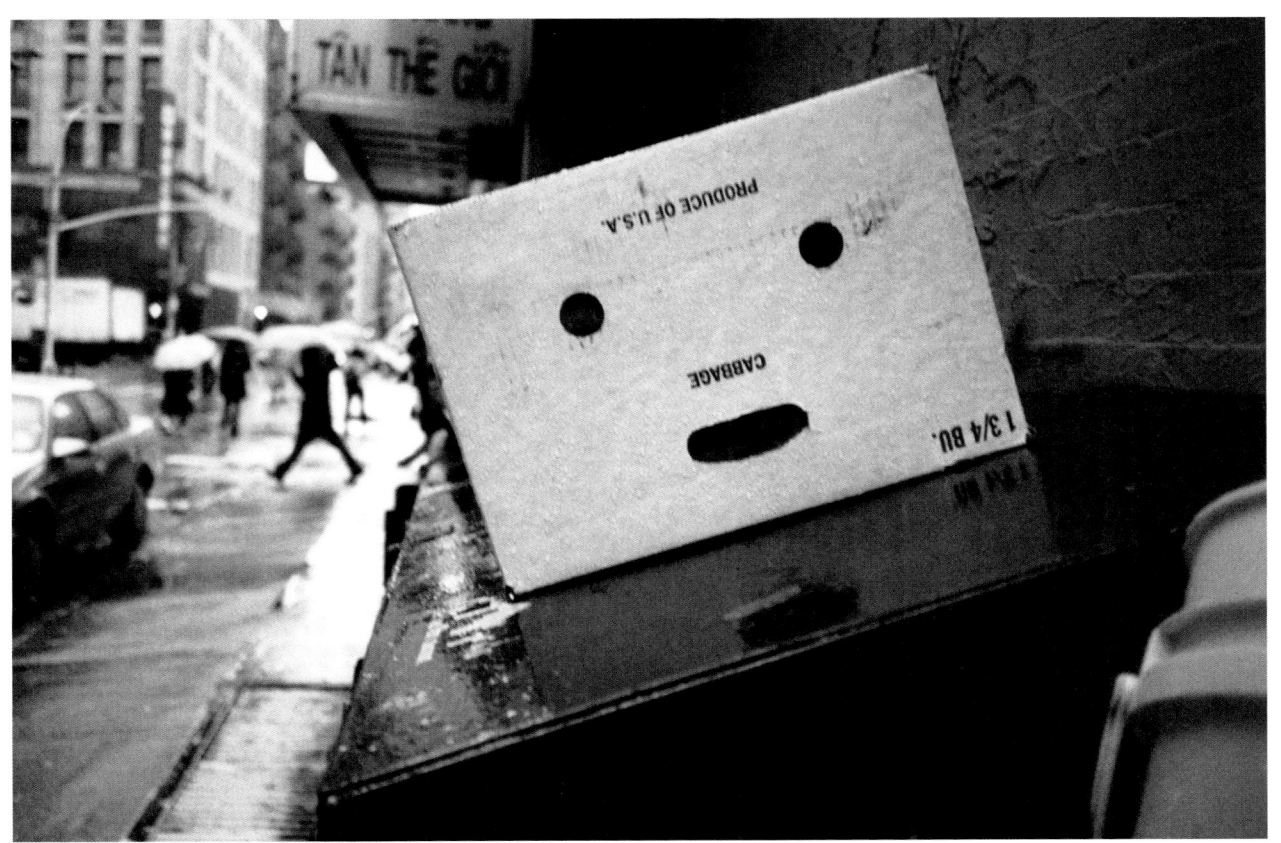

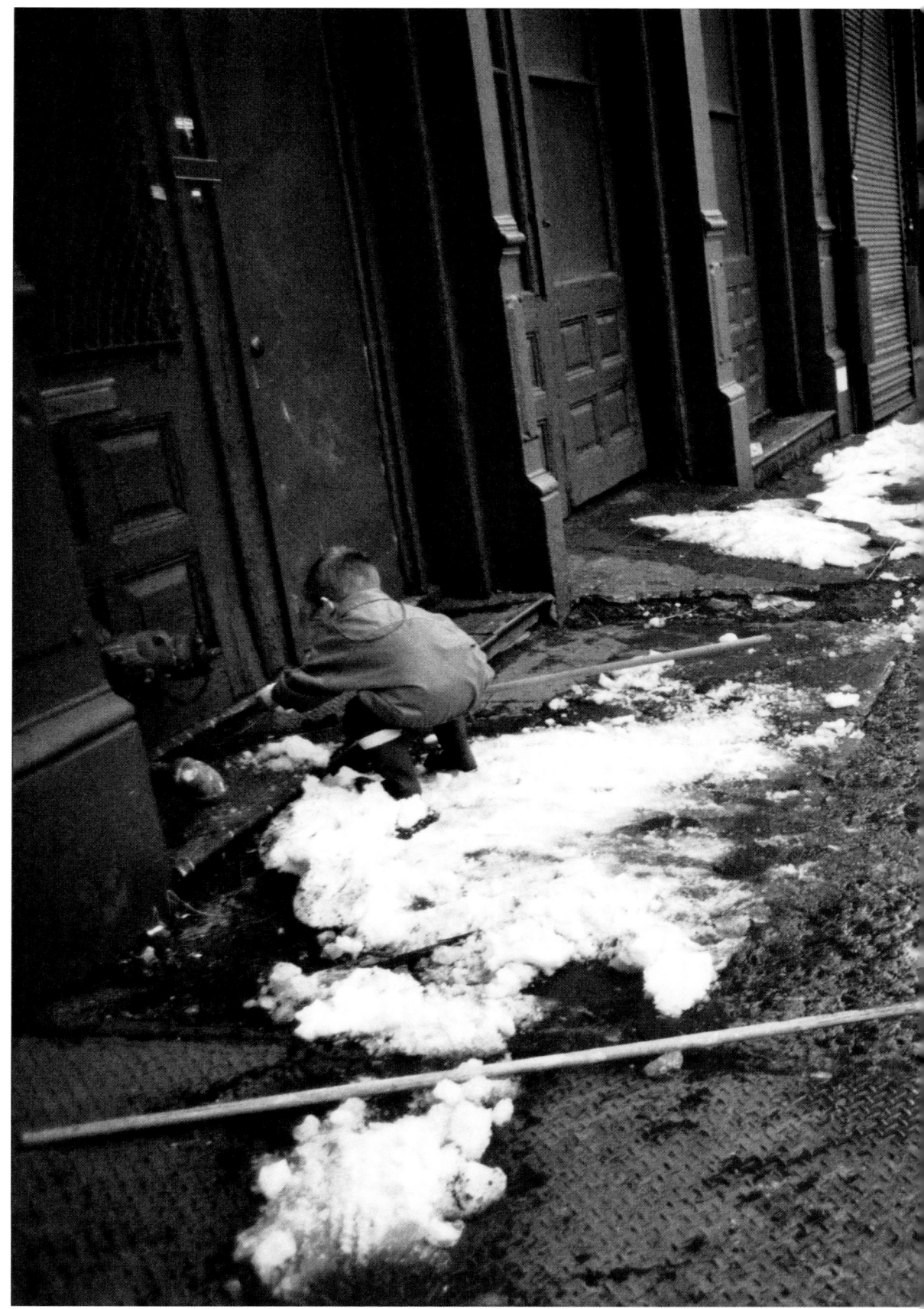

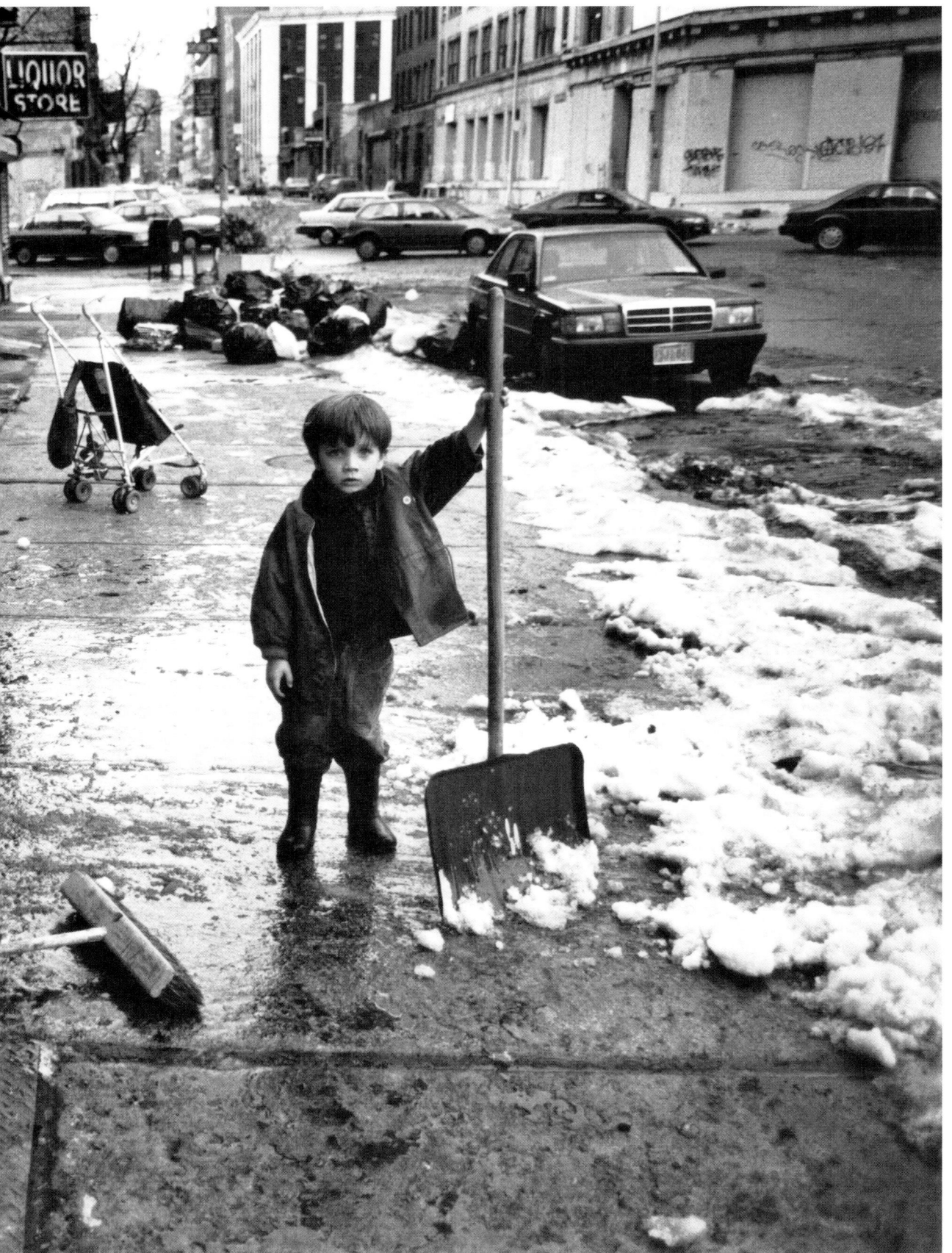

TWO WAY STREET
PART II

As a street photographer, I am always on the hunt for moments that transcend. In "Street Abstractions" these moments are naturally occurring compositions brought to life by light and happenstance. When these images are removed from their environment, they dissociate from representation and become color studies, geometry, shapes, textures, and symbols. I try to leave just enough in the frame to convey something about the scene, but not so much that the scene is the overriding impression of the image. These images owe much to abstract painting but reside squarely in the fleeting moments that are unique to photography.

"Gretchen Grace's street photographs reveal a maze of shape and color within the city's orderly grid."

—John Leland, *New York Times*, March 10, 2019

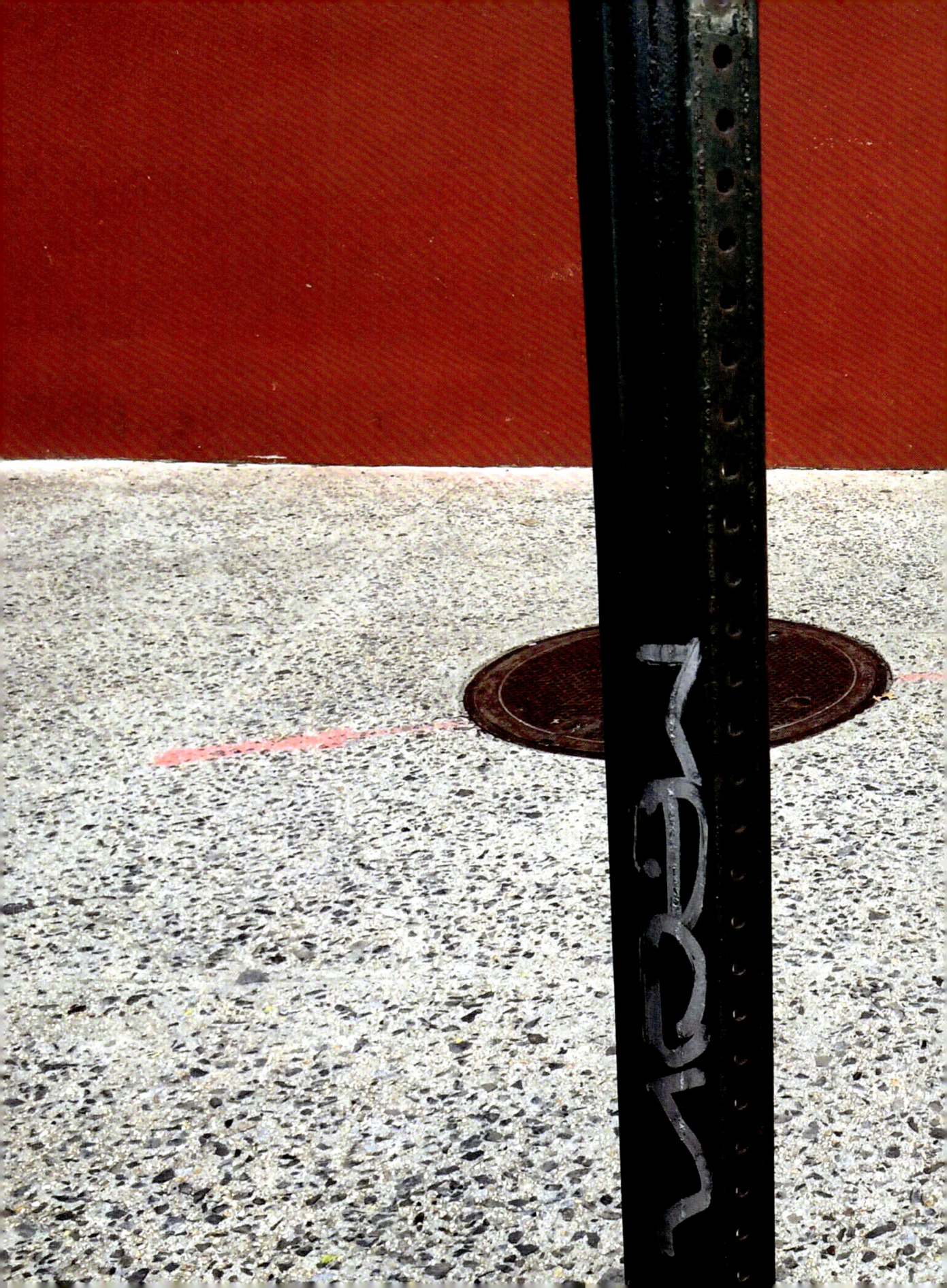

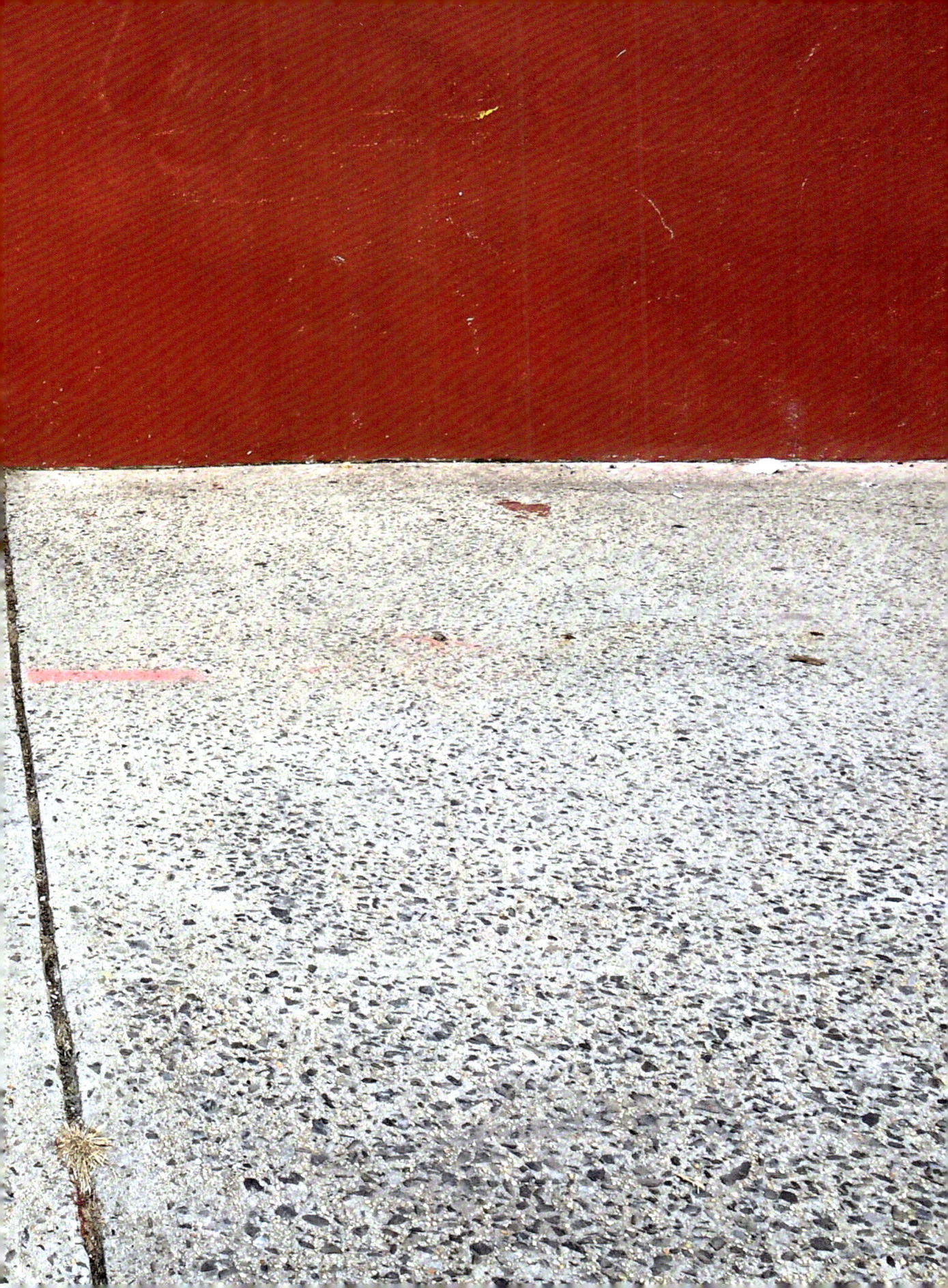

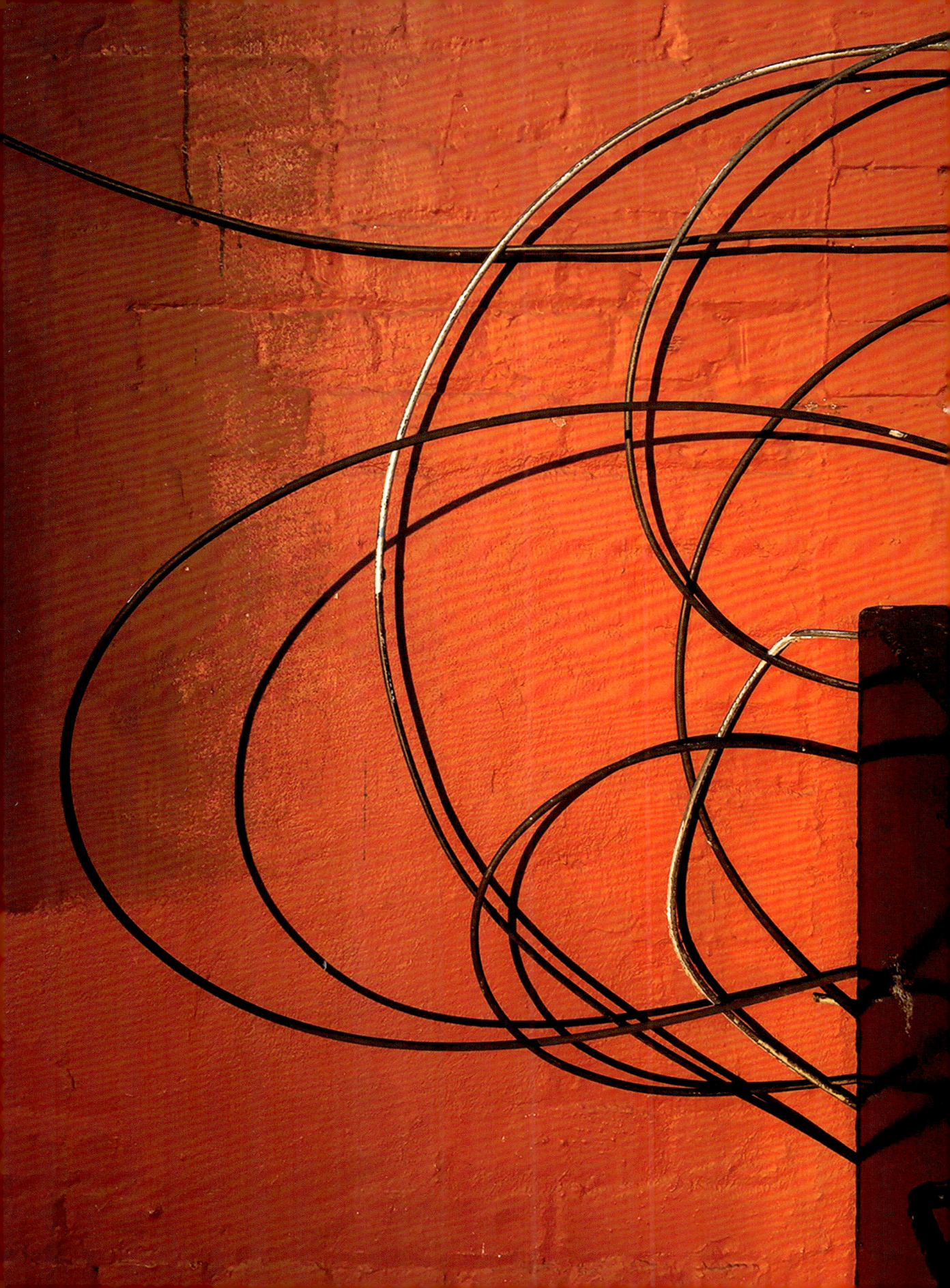

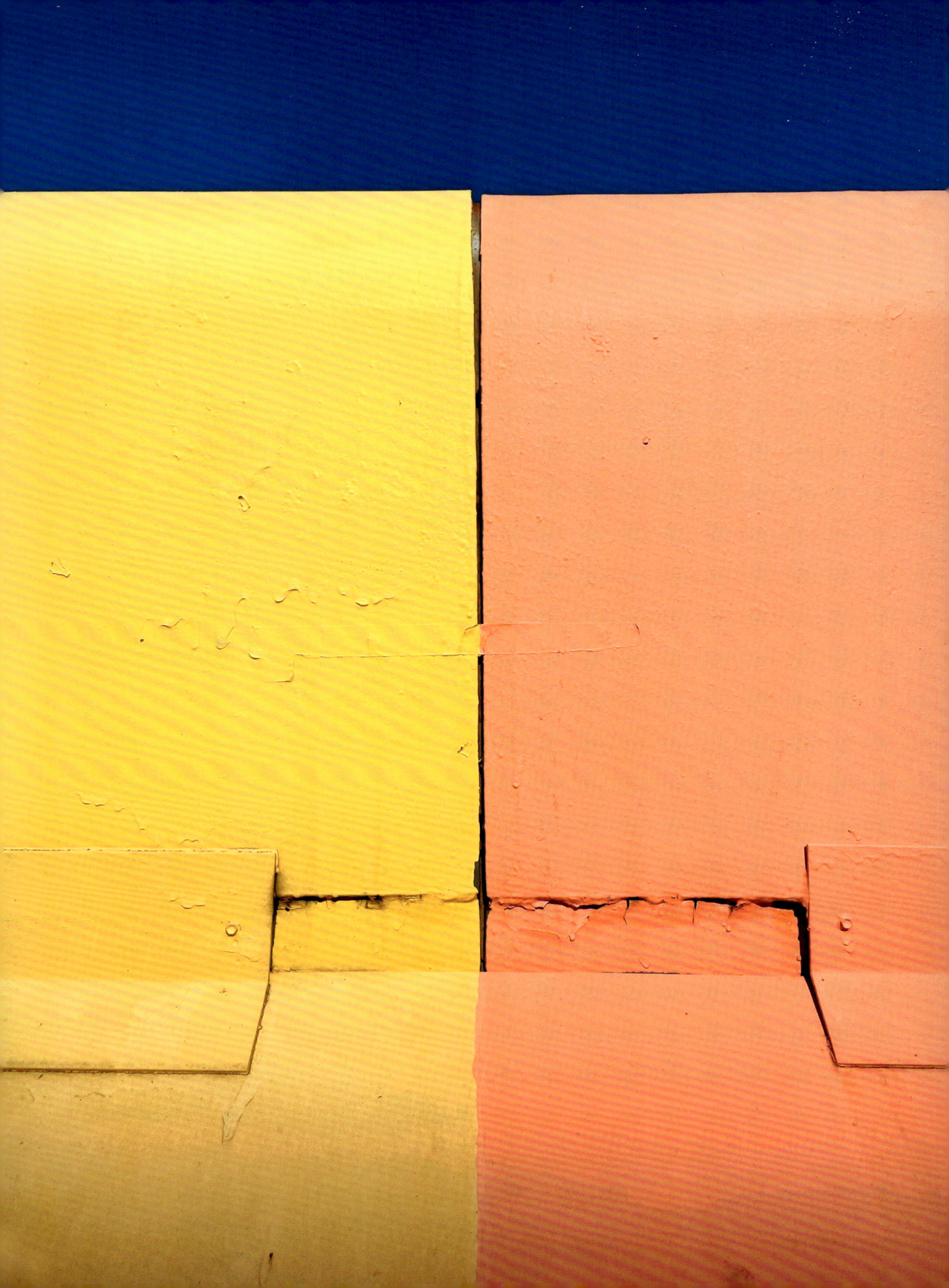

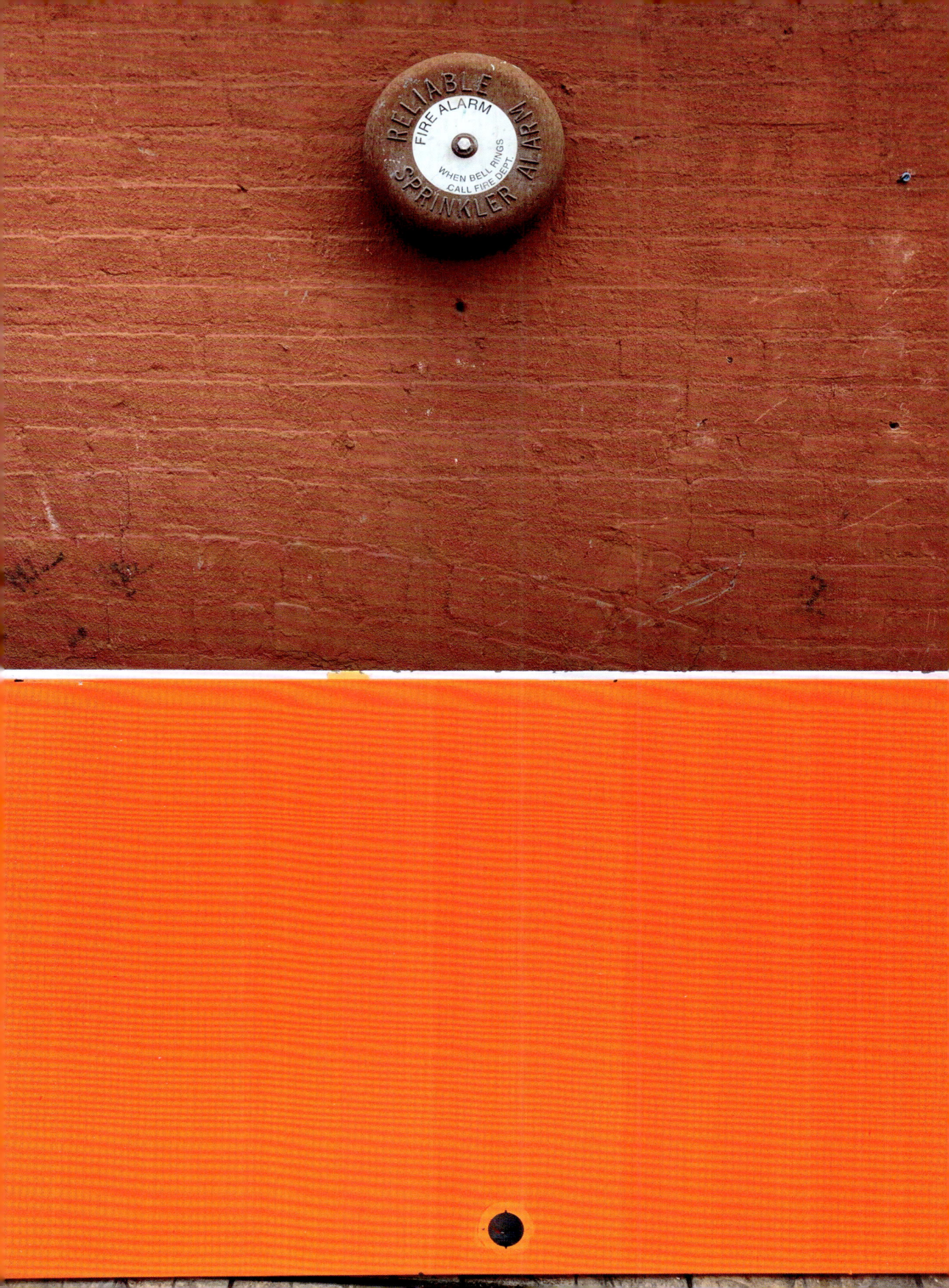

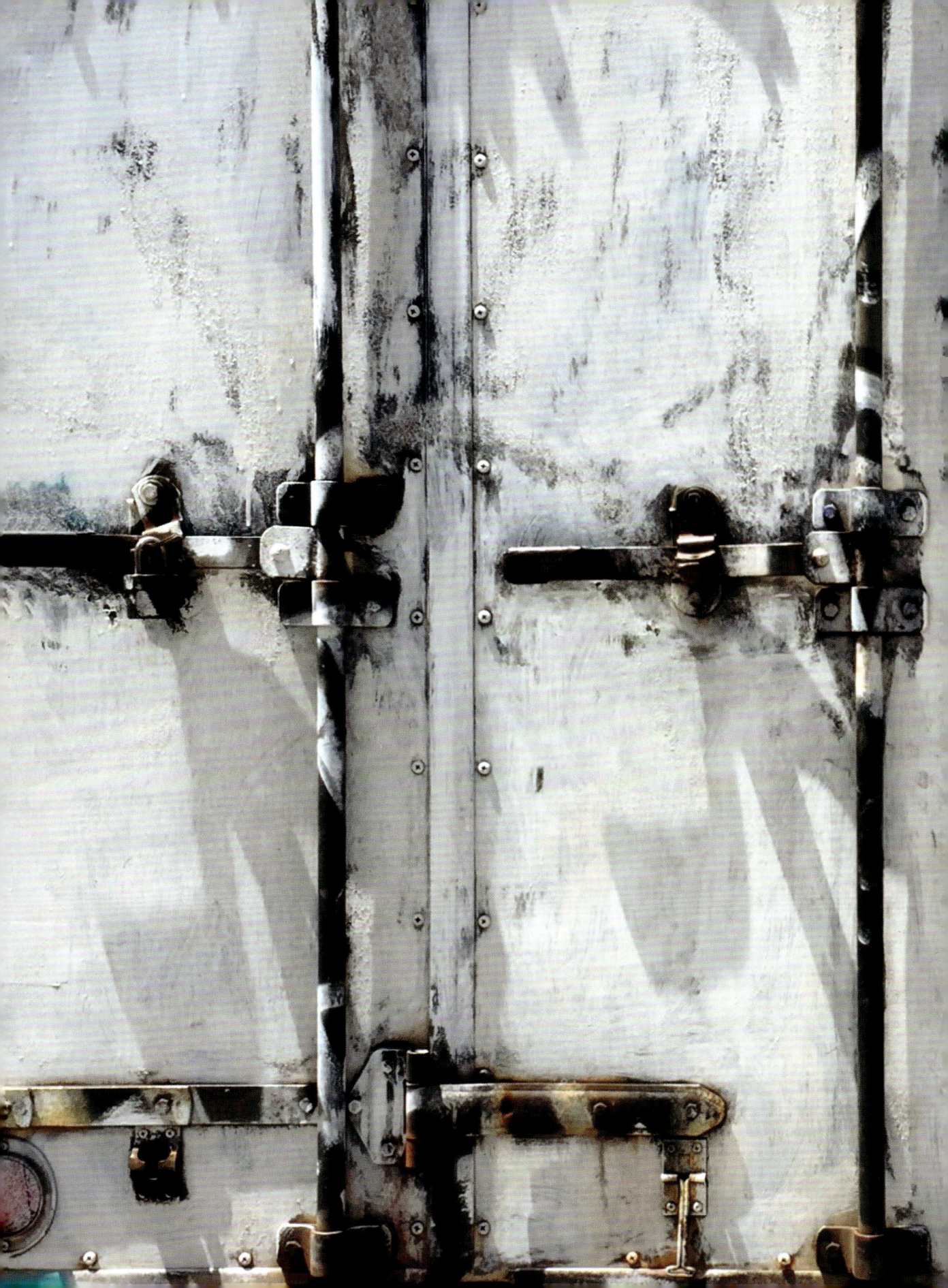

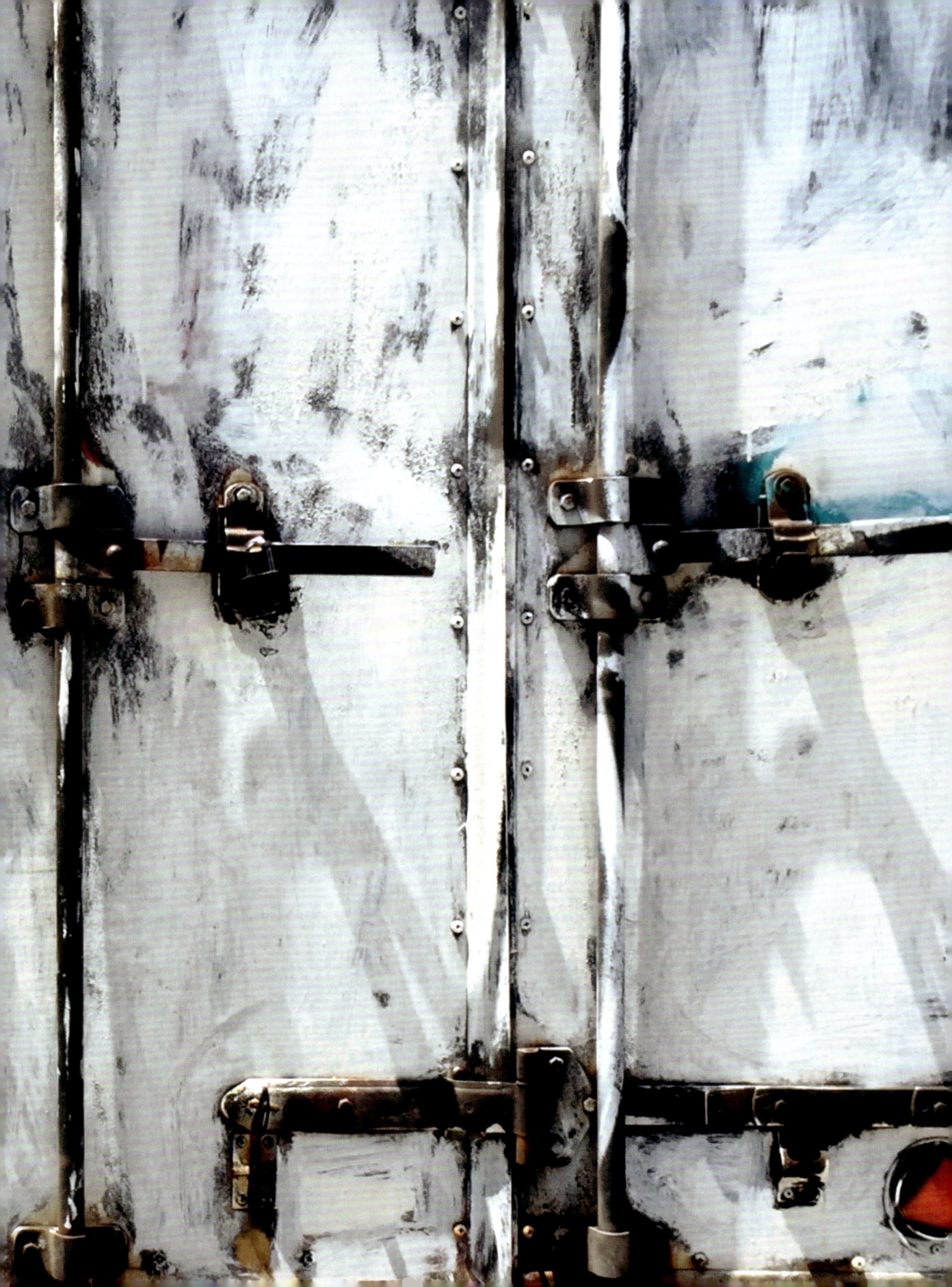

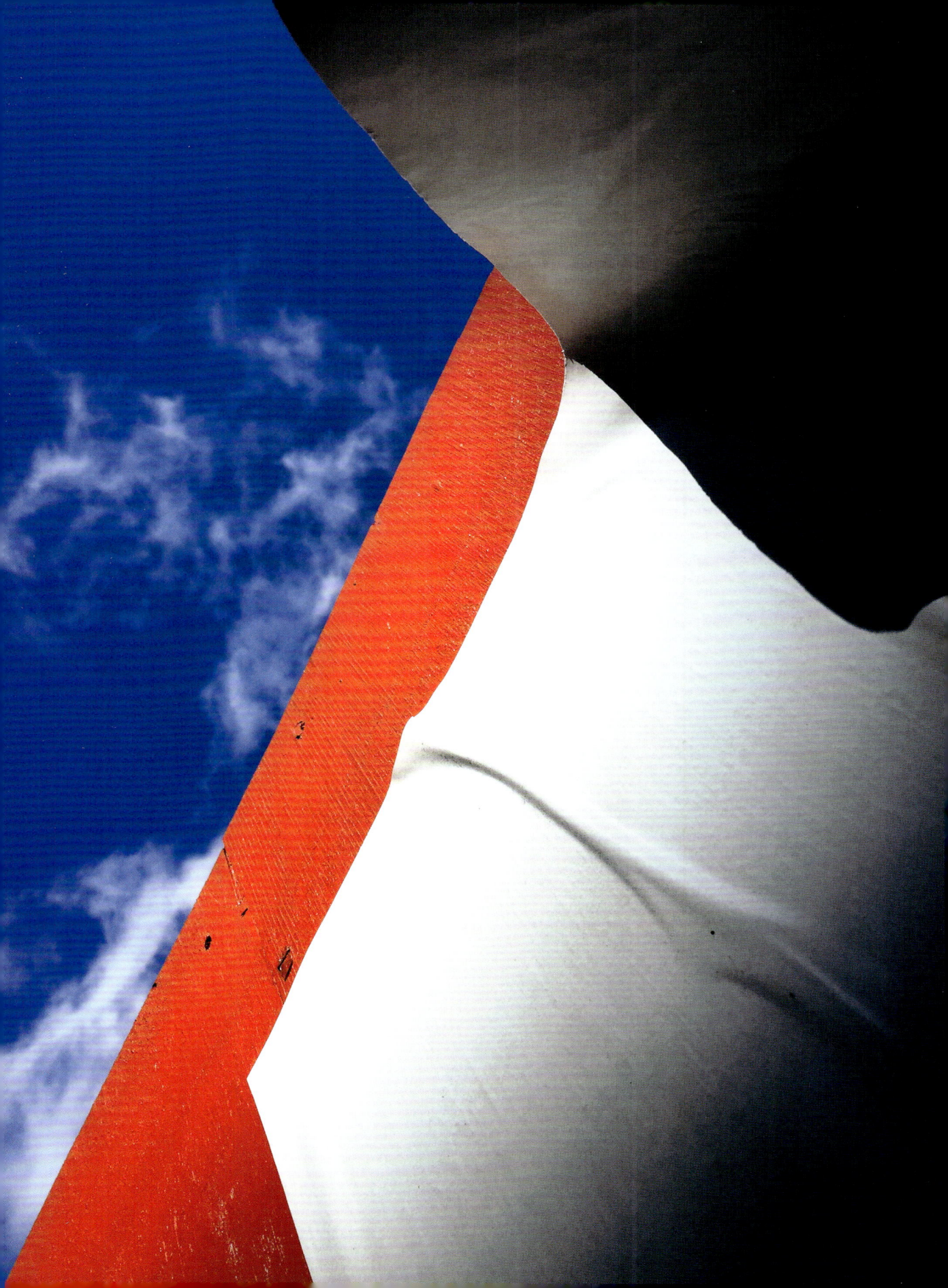

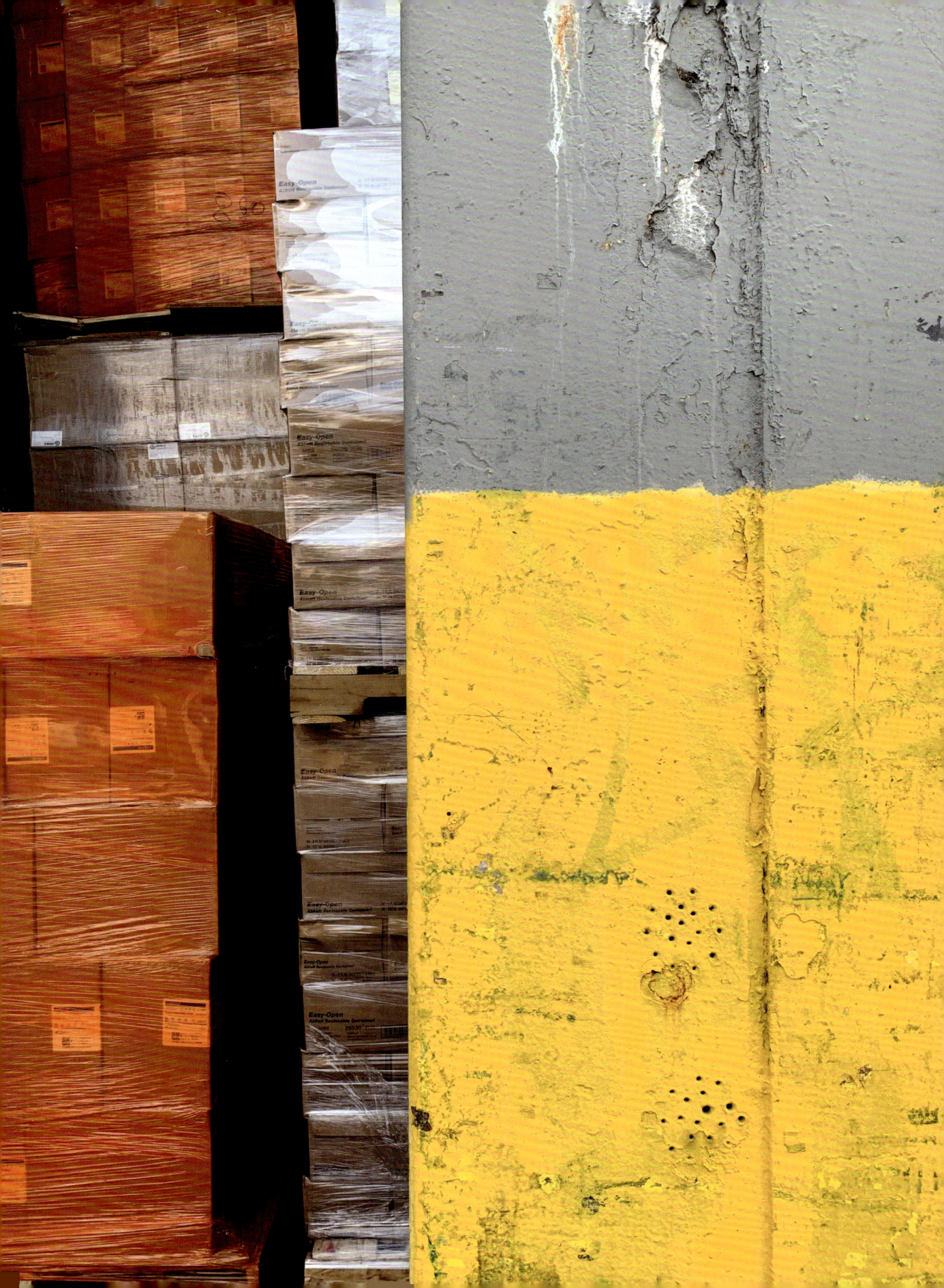

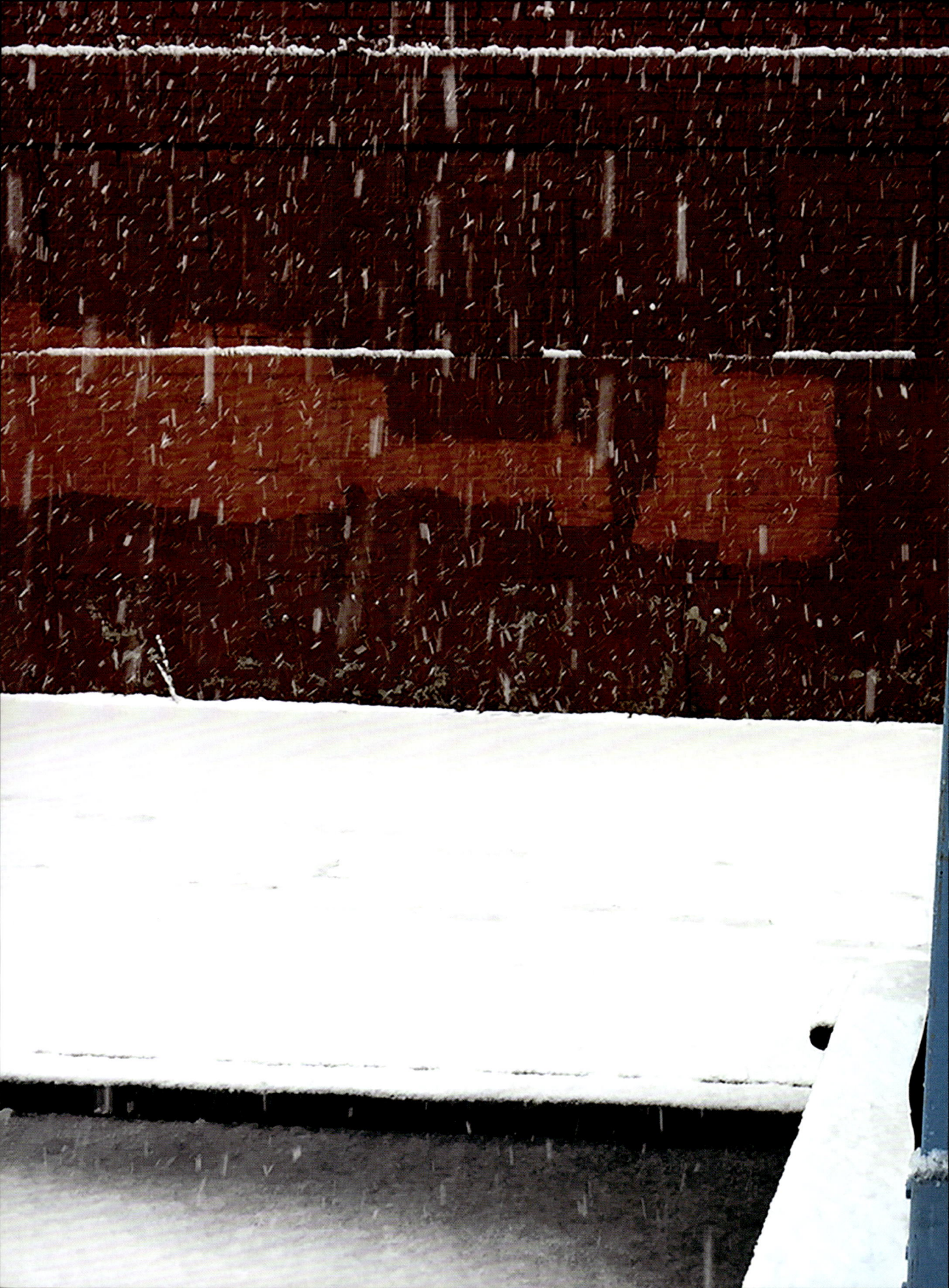

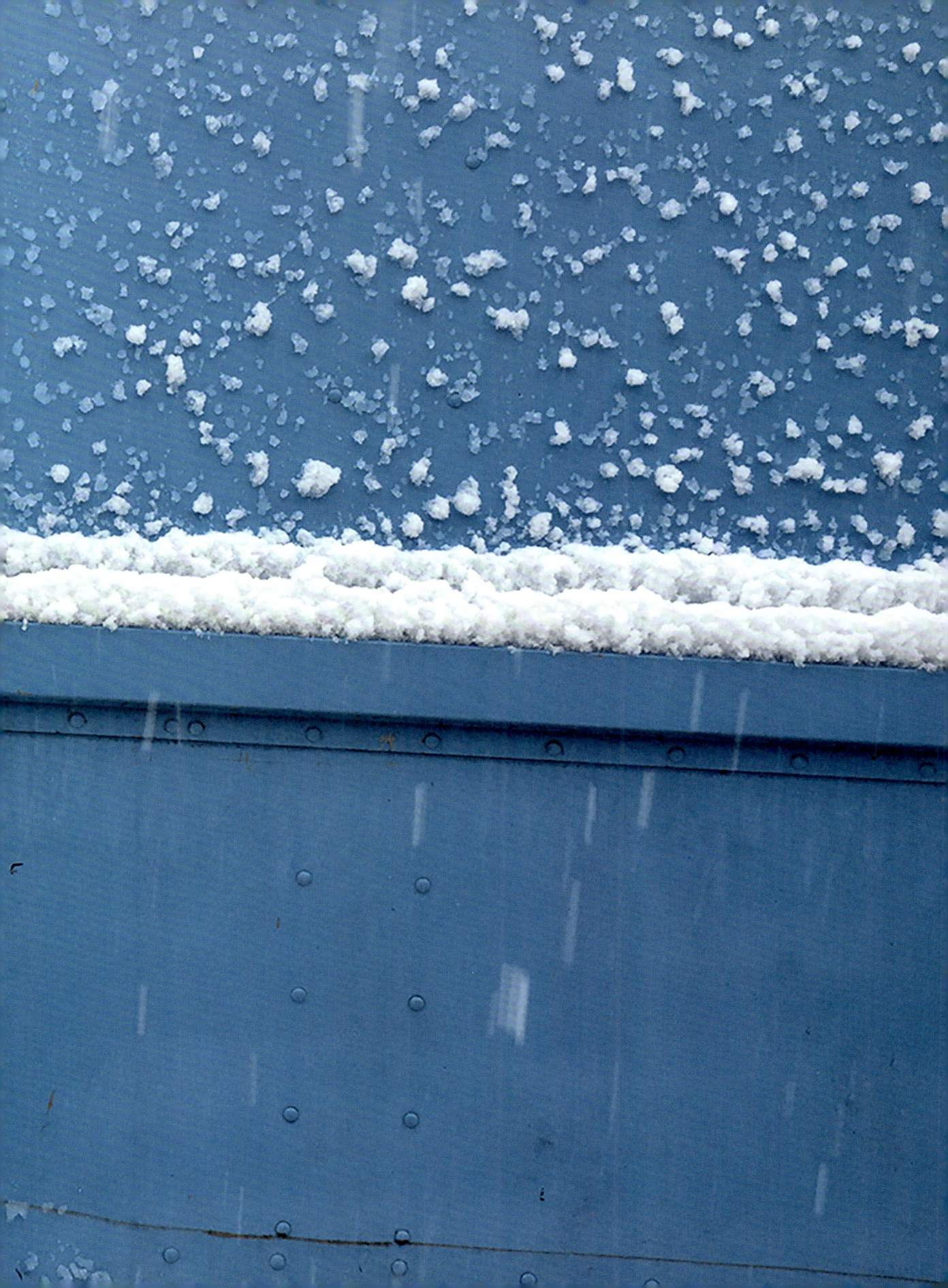

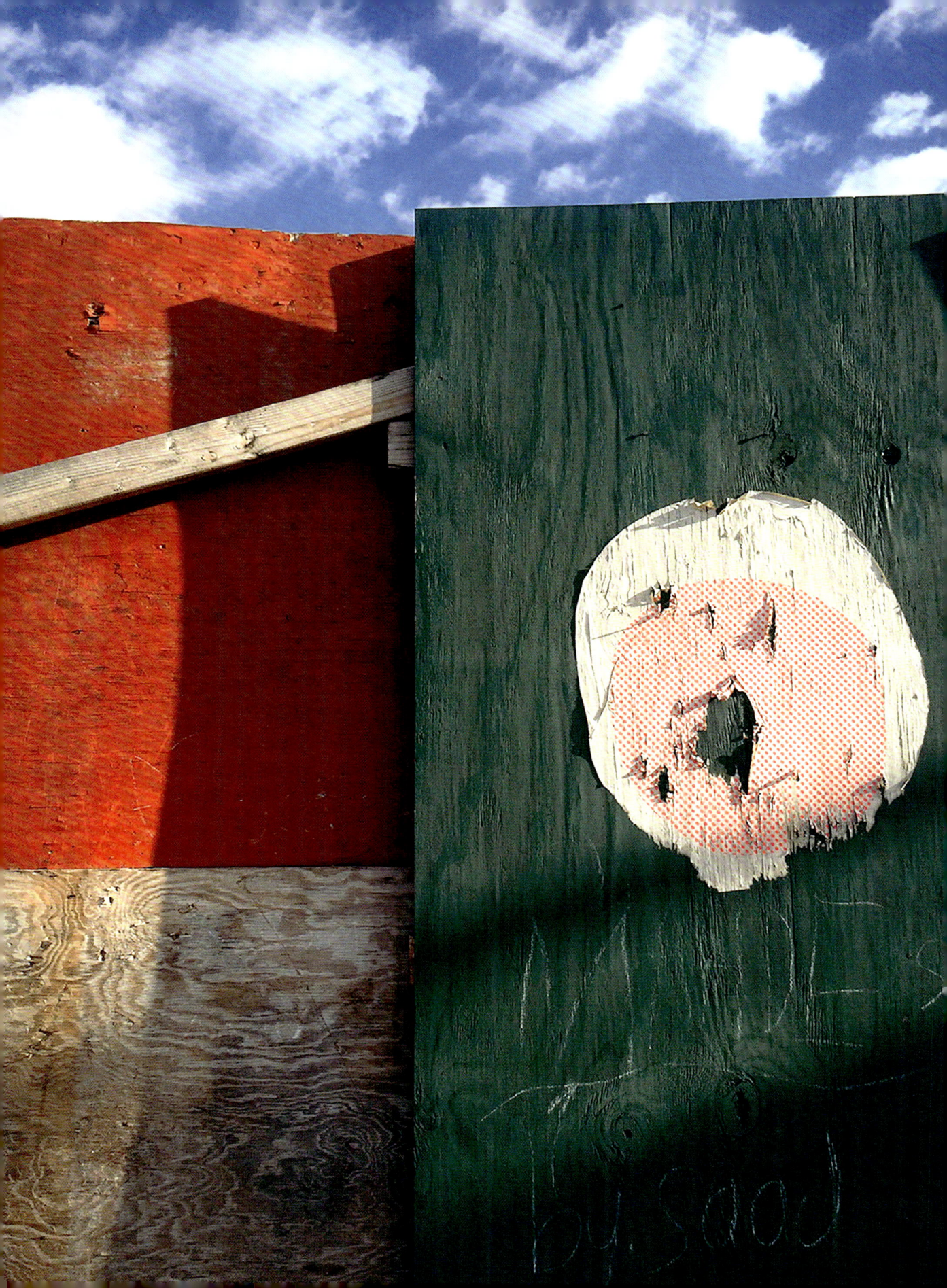

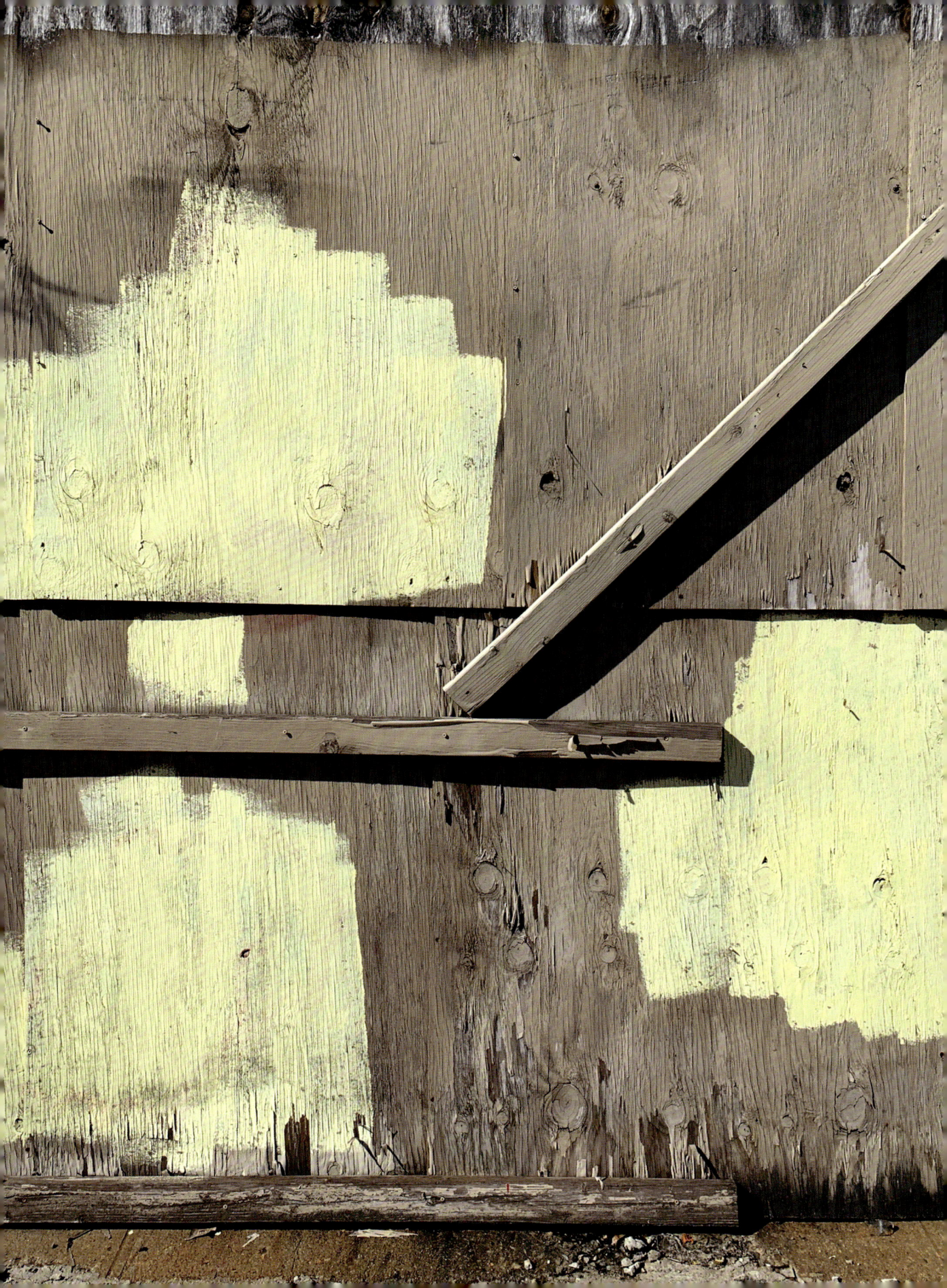

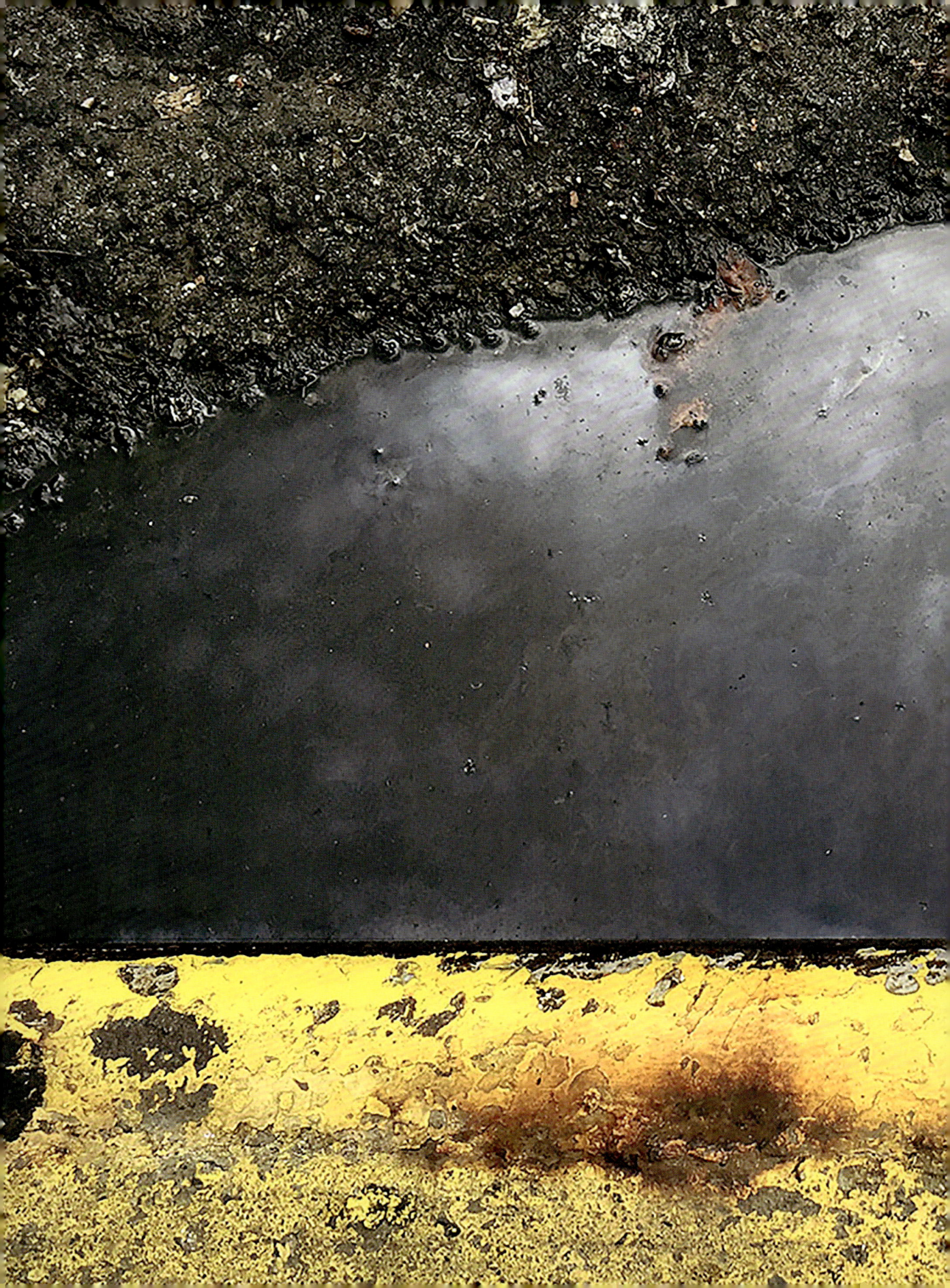

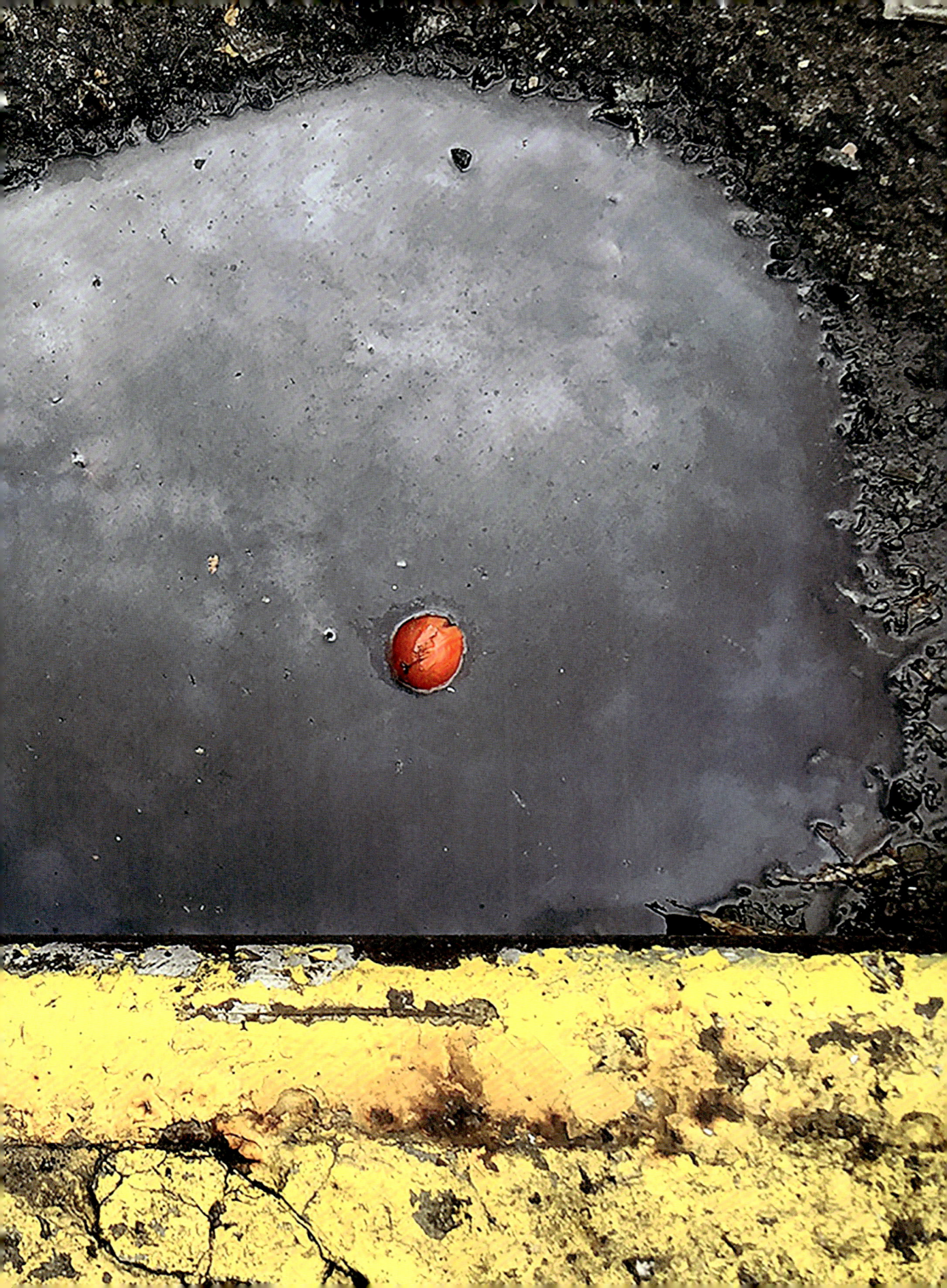

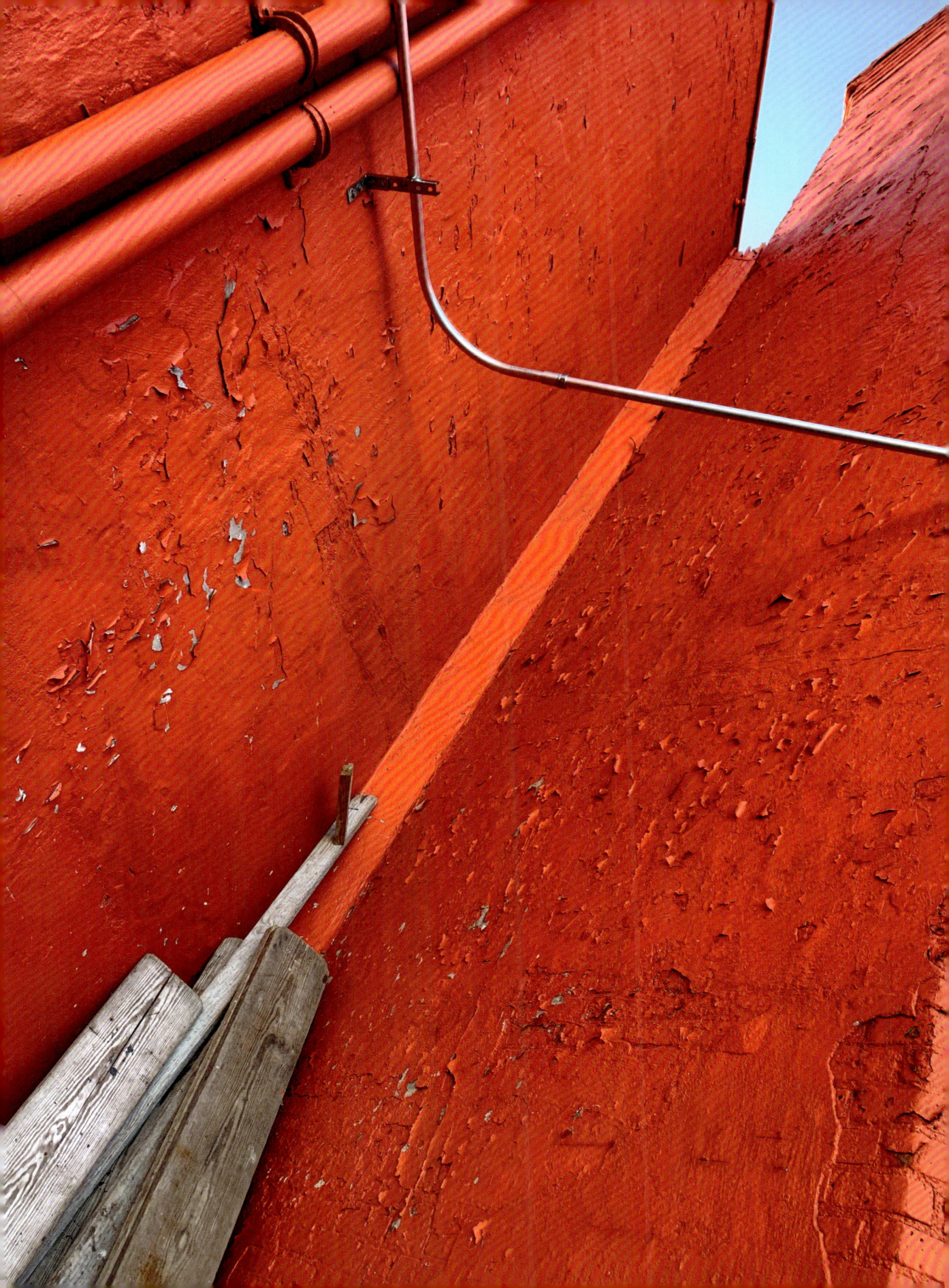

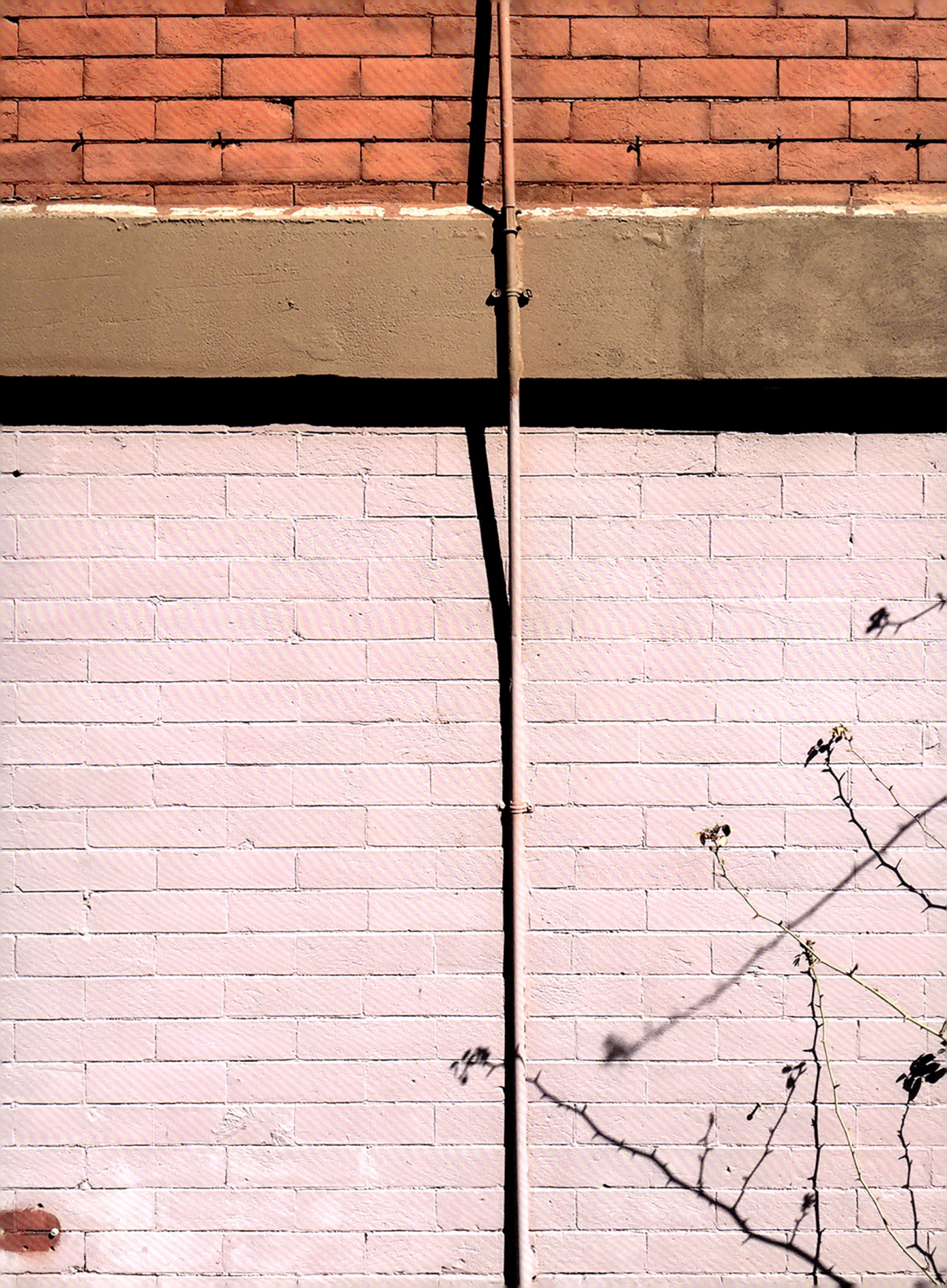

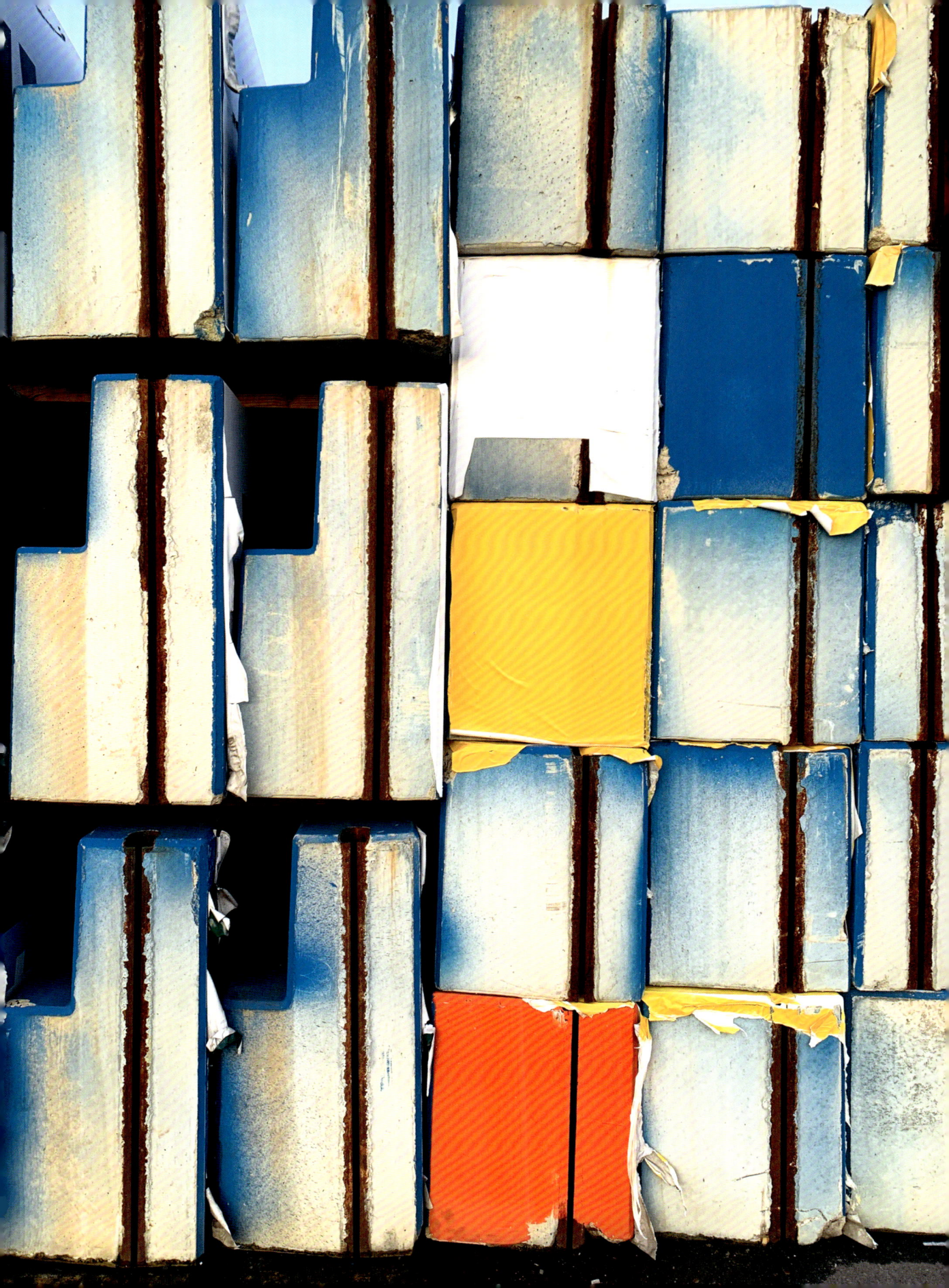

PLATELIST

AFTERWORD

To spend time with Gretchen Grace's photographs is akin to having the privilege of walking through New York City with her, something that I have been lucky enough to do for over thirty years. She sees the city and its people with an incisive wit, a clarity, humor, and humanity. She goes for the indecisive moment, for those in-between times when things are a bit off-kilter. She brings her designer's eye to the images she makes, using the framing as a way to underscore the moment.

This collection of photos is a love letter to New York as it both changes and stays the same. It challenges you to look closely, to not miss the quiet spaces, the subtle human connections, the beauty of the passing light, or the juxtapositions of colors and textures. Her more recent color work feels both new and of a piece with her black-and-white street images. This is work about looking. And finding the unnoticed beauty in the hidden corners of the city. The ones we all walk right past.

Gretchen's work prods us to keep our eyes and hearts open. To stay generous and curious and appreciative. I am grateful for the time that I get to spend with her, and for this reminder.

—Carin Berger

BIOGRAPHIES

Gretchen Grace is a photographer, artist, and designer. For more than thirty years, she has been photographing on the street, in New York City and around the world. For Gretchen, street photography is storytelling, narrative and poetic. Her work is primarily lens based, still and video, real and abstract, and has appeared in publications such as the *New York Times*, *Eyeshot*, *AintBad*, *Smithsonian Magazine*, *Noice*, *Broad*, *Women in Street*, *Strant*, *Daylight*, *Shots*, and *Japan Camera Hunter*.

Julia Coddington practices street and documentary photography. She is a strong advocate for the female voice in street photography, and along with Rebecca Wiltshire, cofounded the Unexposed Collective, a platform and community for Australian women, nonbinary, and intersex street photographers. She is also an administrator of Women in Street, a large international community of women street photographers, and a member of the Little Box Collective, an international collective of street photographers.

Carin Berger is an award-winning designer and the author/illustrator of over a dozen picture books, including *The Little Yellow Leaf*, which was named a New York Times Best Illustrated Book. An obsessive visual curator, she has given talks and led creativity workshops for kids and adults around the world. She is also the founding member of the Pen and Ink Brigade, a group of women activist artists.

ACKNOWLEDGMENTS

Thank you to Michael at Daylight Books for the idea of putting these two bodies of work together in one book, to Ursula for her work bringing the design to life, and to Gabi for her "less is more" approach to editing. Thank you to Junko and Eric at Griffin Editions for their patience and expertise prepping the color images, and to Elizabeth and Jimmy at Picture House and the Small Darkroom for their sensitivity and care printing and scanning the black-and-white film work. To my family and friends who have always been a huge support, both in front of and behind the camera, and to all the strangers who have walked through my frame over the years, I couldn't do this without you. I'm grateful to Julia and Carin for their incisive and beautiful words, to Willa and Everett for their constant inspiration, and to Eric for absolutely everything.